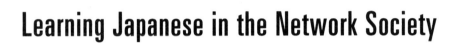

Learning Japanese in the Network Society

Learning Japanese in the Network Society

UNIVERSITY OF
CALGARY
PRESS

Edited by Kazuko Nakajima

University of Calgary Press
2500 University Drive NW
Calgary, Alberta
Canada T2N 1N4
www.uofcpress.com

National Library of Canada Cataloguing in Publication Data

Proceedings of the Second International Conference on Computer Technology and Japanese Language Education, held at the University of Toronto, Aug. 22-25, 1999.

Includes bibliographical references and index.
ISBN 1-55238-070-X

1. Japanese language—Study and teaching—Congresses. 2. Japanese language—Computer-assisted instruction for foreign speakers—Congresses. I. Nakajima, Kazuko.

PL519.L42 2002   495.6   C2002-910098-4

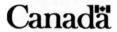
We acknowledge the financial support of the Government of Canada through the Book Publishing Industry Development Program (BPIDP) for our publishing activities.

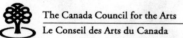
The Canada Council for the Arts
Le Conseil des Arts du Canada

University of Calgary Press gratefully acknowledges the financial support of the Japan Foundation Publication Assistance Programs.

Printed and bound in Canada by Friesens.
∞This book is printed on acid-free paper.

Page, cover design, and typesetting by Kristina Schuring.
Story on the cover is *From the Underground of Jerusalem* taken from the Komatsu Sakyo Corpus <http://castelj.soken.ac.jp/groups/komatsu/>

Acknowledgments   vii

Introduction   viii
    Kazuko Nakajima

Part I   Language Learning in the Network Society

    1   Using Multimedia in the Network Society   1
         Kanji Akahori

    2   Developing CALL Software   25
         Michio Tsutsui

Part II   Database-Supported Language Education

    3   A Gradual Approach to
         Technology-Based Instruction   41
         Hilofumi Yamamoto

    4   Analyzing Japanese Textbooks Using the
         Vocabulary and Kanji Level Checker   71
         Yoshiko Kawamura

    5   Internet-Based Self-Assessment for
         Language Skills   89
         Yasu-Hiko Tohsaku and Hilofumi Yamamoto

Part III Learner Autonomy and Academic
          Language Learning

    6   Learning Through Target Language Texts   105
         Jim Cummins

7 Audio Tapes for the Shinsho Library:
Self-Study Reading Materials   123
Yoko Suzuki, Hiroko Chinen Quackenbush,
and Yuri Shimizu

8 Teaching Heritage Language:
Individualized Learning   145
Masako O. Doulgas

Part IV Collaboration and Copyright

9 Copyright in Japan and Distribution of
the CASTEL/J Database   173
Akifumi Oikawa

Contributors   191
Index   197

Acknowledgments

This book grew out of the Second International Conference on Computer Technology and Japanese Language Education, 22–25 August 1999, held at the University of Toronto. My first and foremost thanks go to my colleagues in the CASTEL/J Research Group, especially the members of the organizing committee of the conference: Yukihiro Komatsu, Masaharu Sakayauchi, and Ryohei Yoshioka of the National Institute for Educational Research, Tokyo; Yukiko Kano and Hirofumi Yamamoto of the University of Tsukuba, Tsukuba, Ibaragi; and Yoko Suzuki of the International Christian University Mitaka, Tokyo. I am also deeply indebted to my friends and distinguished colleagues at the University of Toronto: David Crandfield, Principal of New College, Jim Cummins of OISE, and Ian Lancashire, Director, Centre for Computing in the Humanities. Their encouragement and support have been my source of inspiration and strength to complete this project.

I have been blessed with the warm and generous support of the Shoyu Club Foundation, Tokyo, which made possible the conference and the publication of this book. It is therefore my pleasant duty to acknowledge my utmost gratitude to the president and managing director of the foundation.

My very special thanks go to John Parry, my thoughtful—and ruthless—copy editor, associated with the University of Toronto Press. Without his kind assistance, the completion of this book would simply have not been possible.

Finally, I should like to express my heartfelt gratitude to my husband, Takehide Nakajima, for his untiring support and encouragement.

Kazuko Nakajima
February, 2002

Introduction

Kazuko Nakajima

CASTEL/J and the University of Toronto Conference

Almost fifteen years ago, I started exploring the seemingly unlimited potential for applying computer technology to language instruction. While teaching Japanese as a foreign language in the Department of East Asian Studies at the University of Toronto, I became painfully aware that a four-year university program did not adequately prepare students to use a learned language for graduate studies or the workplace. My colleagues and I faced a constant dilemma: the time and resources available at university to learn Japanese were limited, yet Japanese is one of the four most difficult languages in the world, according to the Foreign Service Institute of the U.S. State Department. Students and faculty members in other fields such as Japanese literature, Japanese history, and the social sciences had unrealistic assumptions about how quickly students could acquire even a working knowledge of Japanese.

I had from the start a special interest in using computer communications to promote writing skills through "authentic" peer interactions between my students here in Canada and native speakers of Japanese in Japan. E-mail exchanges using Japanese scripts and videoconferencing are now a way of life but were like a dream fifteen years ago. A gift of Xerox Star multilingual text-processing workstations, donated in 1986 through a Xerox University Grant, allowed me to initiate a bilingual e-mail exchange program in collaboration with Professor Hiroshi Suzuki of the University of Tokyo. His students majoring in international relations wrote e-mail in English, their weaker language, and my students wrote back in Japanese, their new language. The vehicle for these interactions was a computer-assisted writing course in Japanese or Chinese, which our department first offered in 1987. Many students benefited greatly from this innovative approach and established friendships with their electronic penpals. The presence of distant but real audiences transformed the learning of literacy skills in Japanese from a passive to an active process.

I had a keen interest also in applying technological innovations to help students acquire the Chinese characters, or kanji, used in Japanese. To become able to read a Japanese text of substantial content, such as a newspaper article, usually requires a serious English-speaking student five or six years of intensive study. With the support of Apple Canada and the Apple Canada Education Foundation, my computer site in our department was in 1987 designated the Apple Centre for Innovation in East Asian Languages. With Kanji-Macintosh microcomputers, and also the very generous support of the Donner Canadian Foundation from 1989 to 1992, I developed kanji-learning software called KanjiCard using the HyperCard program on an early version of Macintosh computers (System 2.3).

Since 1990, I have been participating in Japan's CASTEL/J Research Group (Computer Assisted System of Teaching and Learning/Japanese) as a research associate from Canada. This pioneering endeavour planned to develop an instructional multimedia database for Japanese. My association with the research group led me to organize the Second International Conference on Computer Technology and Japanese Language Education, which took place at the University of Toronto, 22–25 August 1999. The conference —which attracted three times as many participants as its 1997 predecessor in Pavia, Italy—brought together practitioners and researchers of computer-assisted language learning (CALL) and Japanese language pedagogy and linguistics, as well as experts from educational technology, cognitive science, second language acquisition, and linguistics.

The conference featured three keynote addresses, over fifty papers on various topics including development of Internet-based instructional materials and experiments with and evaluation of practical technology applications, a panel discussion on multimedia digital courseware, and hands-on workshops. It also gave educators and scholars from across North America their first close look at the wide range of databases and tools for learning Japanese contained in CASTEL/J on CD-ROM. The conference's primary purpose was to promote research in CALL, as well as technology-enhanced and database-supported language instruction, particularly in teaching and learning Japanese as a foreign, or second, or heritage language (JFL, JSL, or JHL, respectively). The event gave researchers and practitioners a chance to coordinate their efforts and to plan for future collaboration.

The conference brought together specialists in computer science, information technology, and cognitive science, who knew little or nothing about language teaching, and specialists in Japanese language pedagogy, who tended to lack knowledge about state-of-the-art technology. Specialists within Japan met specialists elsewhere; the two groups had not until then effectively communicated or shared experiences. People espousing traditional and current concepts about language instruction learned about emerging technological innovations of the twenty-first century. It quickly became clear that our discoveries about recent and continuing changes in language learning were important enough to share in book form.

There has been a sea change in language instruction. During the past few decades, exciting technological advances have led language teachers to develop a new set of teaching paradigms. For example, in the 1960s audiolingual and audiovisual methods emerged in tandem with audiovisual technology. Educational institutions throughout the world equipped language labs with tape recorders, microphones, headsets, and televisions. More recent "interactive" language learning uses computers and computer-mediated communication.

What will the coming "network society" bring? This question is central to this book and generates many lines of inquiry. Where does language learning go from here? What new teaching practices will develop? How will they differ from traditional practices? What new roles will teachers and educational institutions play in foreign language education? What about new curricula, classroom activities, and instructional materials? How will technology help learners to acquire literacy or reading skills? How will we assess and evaluate learners' performances? Can technology accelerate the learning of kanji, for example? What of the ethics of sharing the abundant resources available on the Internet?

During the conference, participants offered some tentative answers and focused on four themes that shape this book: language learning in the network society, database-supported language education, learner's autonomy and academic language learning; and collaboration and copyright.

Japanese as a Model?

Eleanor H. Jorden (2000) reported recently that the Foreign Service Institute of the U.S. State Department "has divided the languages of the world into four categories, depending on how many hours of formal study each required, on the average, for an American to achieve a designated level of oral proficiency." Category 4 consists of Japanese, Chinese, Korean, and Arabic. They are "the most difficult [languages] for native speakers of English...." For the average American learner, these languages required approximately four times as long to reach a given level as a language in Category 1, which included the languages of Western Europe.

Jorden further observes that:

> learning Japanese is *not* like learning Spanish. It was estimated that level 3, or Superior, according to the guidelines set by the American Council for Teachers of Foreign Languages (ACTFL), required approximately twenty-five hundred hours of instruction or two years of a thirty-hour-per-week program. Nothing in academia came close. Even using the narrowed ACTFL levels, learners in academia were often at the same level when they completed a Japanese language course as they had been when they entered it. Few could ever reach the Advanced level, much less the Superior, within an academic course of study. (p. 2)

After mentioning the Proficiency and Prochievement movements in the 1980s and the Standards-based movement in the 1990s, Jorden asked the conference members, "Do you suppose that if all these movements had started with Japanese, we might have suggested a more generally useful approach, moving in areas that are of much broader significance?" She quoted A. Ronald Walton:

> I would suggest that ACTFL ... begin, this time, with the LCTLs [less commonly taught languages] and work into the Indo-European languages rather than the other way around, a procedure that hind-

sight reveals would have made more sense with all of the ACTFL ILR Guidelines. (p. 6) [The ILR is the Interagency Language Round-table of the U.S. State Department.]

This book discusses common issues of computer technology and language education shared by teachers and learners of foreign, second, and heritage languages. *Learning Japanese in the Network Society* may shed light on what language learning paradigms will work best as new paradigms in language education in the next century. I suggest Japanese as a model precisely because it is one of the most difficult languages to learn to speak, to read, and to write. Its writing system is often described as one of the most complicated in the world, and its writing style is much more elliptical than that of western European languages. Moreover, Japanese, once considered an "exotic" language, has become one of the world's most-used foreign languages. According to a recent survey conducted by the Japan Foundation in 1998, while English now ranks first for international business and politics, education, and academic research, Japanese ranks second in many countries, especially in much of East Asia.

A Quick Primer of the Japanese Language

Acquiring oral proficiency in Japanese is as daunting for English speakers as learning written Japanese, primarily because of socio-cultural factors, for instance, the language's sophisticated "honorific" system. A speaker of Japanese must select an appropriate register, exalted or humble, depending on his or her relationship with the addressee in terms of social status, age, and gender.

Students, however, face an even greater challenge in learning written Japanese because they must learn two disparate orthographies, phonetic kana syllabaries and logographic or ideographic kanji, in addition to roman letters or romaji. Roman letters are used mainly for street names and signs to help foreign visitors in Japan, and are now also used to type characters on computers. There are two kana syllabaries, hiragana and katakana, each representing forty-six basic syllables. They were developed in Japan and are based on ancient kanji characters. Hiragana scripts are currently used to transcribe the inflectional parts of sentences such as verb inflections, suffixes, and postpositions, while katakana are employed mainly for words of foreign origin such as "coffee," "taxi," computer terms, and onomatopoeic words. Kanji characters are used for transcribing content words such as nouns and verb stems wherever there are relevant kanji.

Kanji originated more than three thousand years ago as "hanzi," which means "letters of the *Han* dynasty of China." Since the Japanese adopted kanji in about the fifth century A.D., major phonological changes have altered the characters, but their shape and basic form have been surprisingly stable. Unlike Chinese and Korean, in which a Chinese character generally has a one-to-one relationship with a sound, kanji have multiple readings which depend on the context. This is the result of the acquired habit of reading each kanji in two ways—the way the Chinese read hanzi, as well as the way the Japanese read kanji. Alluding to Roman mythology, Takao Suzuki (1978) called this dual system "Janus" (a god who has two faces) and considers it one of the major reasons why Chinese characters are so deeply rooted in the Japanese language. The commonly used kanji for printing and education consists of 1,985 kanji characters, with 3,406 readings. In visual processing of kanji, the reader may often understand its meaning but not necessarily know how to pronounce it.

Learning kanji is such an onerous task that even a native school child in Japan normally requires nine years to learn them, despite daily exposure to television, posters, and street signs. To learn how to write an individual kanji character is a very involved process: a student must learn first how many strokes a character contains and then in what order to combine them. The average number of strokes in "basic curriculum kanji," according to Kaiho and Nomura (1983), is 9.4, whereas that of the roman alphabet is only 2.0. A student must learn several readings of a kanji and is expected to discriminate one from another on the basis of context. He or she must also learn exactly which part of a single word should be written in kanji characters and which part in other phonetic scripts—hiragana and katakana. These factors make it extremely strenuous and time-consuming to write a kanji, if not a sentence, as neatly and accurately as expected.

Both instructors and students tend to be so involved with the learning and teaching of individual kanji that they pay very little attention to the idea or content of the writing. Because the cultural traits of how ideas are organized in the oriental way are drastically different from the western way, interpreting content is another hurdle to developing reading and writing skills. R.B. Kaplan (1966), who analyzed some seven hundred foreign students' compositions in twenty languages, including Japanese, Chinese, and Korean, compares oriental writing with that in English:

> An English expository paragraph usually begins with a topic statement, and then, by a series of subdivisions so that topic statement, each supported by example and illustrations, proceeds to develop that central idea and relate that idea to all the other ideas in the whole essay, and to employ that idea in its proper relationship with the other ideas, to prove something, or perhaps to argue something. Some oriental writing, on the other hand, is marked by what may be called an approach by indirection. (pp. 4–5)

Kaplan later continues:

> … the subject is never looked at directly. Things are developed in terms of what they are not, rather than in terms of what they are…. Such a development in a modern English paragraph would strike the English reader as awkward and unnecessarily indirect (p. 10).

It is the reader's responsibility, not the author's, to find out what the author means.

All these factors make it inevitable that foreign students will develop inhibitions and negative attitudes towards writing in Japanese.

Modern Technologies and Learning Japanese

The advent of microcomputers has transformed culture and society in East Asian countries. The Chinese, the Japanese, and the Koreans have never been blessed with a touch typewriter because of the enormous number of characters to be processed in their written language. Joseph Becker (1985), who developed Xerox Star's oriental language software, commented on the situation:

What can be said of an alphabet containing over fifty-thousand letters? If nothing else, it certainly makes a language hard to touch type. The Chinese, Japanese and Korean scripts are based on ancient Chinese ideographic characters, whose vast number has precluded the development of convenient typing devices until quite recently. The advent of the minicomputer has stimulated a technological and social revolution in Asia by making it practical to type Chinese, Japanese and Korean (pp. 1–2).

Teaching writing, until the emergence of microcomputers, was one of the most neglected areas in JFL or JSL. Now Japanese students can create sentences in Japanese on the screen by inputting romaji letters into an ordinary English keyboard. They no longer need to waste time hunting for a correct kanji in a dictionary. They no longer suffer through the demanding process of writing kanji after kanji by hand. The use of microcomputers now allows them to pay more attention to the larger unit, for example, the order of idea presentation.

Emerging technologies are revolutionizing learning Japanese by helping to ease the learning process. Computer-assisted language learning (CALL) applied to kanji learning and literacy development in Japanese is one excellent example of how technologies can make an enormous difference in foreign language learning and teaching. I hope that the research and experiments discussed in this book will inspire further technological applications for language learning, not only in Japanese but also in other languages.

Scope and Outline of the Book

This book tries to strike a balance between theoretical inquiry and practical applications, so it should be of interest to researchers, students and teachers, and school administrators, as well as to general readers.

It covers a wide range of topics—software development (chapters 1 and 2), instructional tools (chapters 3 and 4), Internet-based self-assessment (chapter 5), independent reading (chapters 6 and 7), and individualized learning (chapter 8). In terms of learning environments, it covers JSL for pre-university students (chapter 1), JSL for university and adult students (chapters 2–5 and 7), English as a second language (ESL) at K–12 (chapter 6), and JHL (chapter 8).

Part I of this book (chapters 1 and 2) looks at language learning in the network society. In chapter 1, **Kanji Akahori** outlines the premises of language education in a "network society." He contrasts this with previous "industrial" and "information" societies and describes the research frameworks, evaluation schemes, and problems of the new approach. He presents the various systems and programs that he has developed for experiments with his colleagues and students. These include an interactive multimedia program featuring a popular Japanese film for oral/listening skills (Tsuri-baka Nisshi), web-based comic strips for listening and cultural understanding, and an automatic kanji–hiragana conversion program for Japanese school children outside of Japan.

Michio Tsutsui, in chapter 2, discusses new directions in CALL software, using his program Language Partner as a model. Language Partner is currently available only for improving conversational skills in Japanese, but the principle is applicable to other languages. Tsutsui values technology assessment, usability, expandability, and flexibility in software design and emphasizes user participation in dissemination. To address problems in CALL development, he advocates collaboration among Japanese teaching specialists using a web bulletin board and collaboration with specialists in other disciplines and in other institutions.

Database-supported language education is the theme of Part II (chapters 3–5). In chapter 3, **Hilofumi Yamamoto** presents the theoretical background of database-supported language instruction on the basis of a system of computer-managed instruction (CMI). He describes client-server communication and a calculation system. He introduces tools, such as vocabulary and grammar checkers, that are based on these systems and that are available to instructors through the Internet. He explores the relationship of these systems with curriculum design and classroom teaching through kanji instruction and grammar self-tutorials.

In chapter 4, **Yoshiko Kawamura** describes how she determined the difficulty level of reading materials by using two powerful tools: Vocabulary Level Checker (VLC) and Kanji-Level Checker (KLC). She examines eight existing Japanese language textbooks ranging from elementary to advanced, assessing them in terms of the four levels of the Japan Foundation's Japanese Language Proficiency Test and shows a general correlation between the supposed level of difficulty of a textbook and the difficulty of its vocabulary and kanji. The vlc and klc are now integrated into the award-winning website "Reading Tutor" <http://language.tiu.ac.jp>.

The authors of chapter 5, **Yasu-Hiro Tohsaku** and **Hilofumi Yamamoto,** collaborated in ground-breaking research on Internet-based self-assessment. Their system evaluates language skills according to the rating descriptions of the Interagency Language Roundtable, developed originally to measure the foreign language abilities of U.S. government employees. They assess four skill areas—speaking, listening, reading, and writing—in six levels. The entire process can be executed through or on the Internet by simple steps. Language instructors can use such a tool to place students at an appropriate level, transfer them from program to program, measure their abilities, and compare an individual's ability before and after study abroad.

Part III (chapters 6–8) examines the related issues of learners' autonomy and academic language learning. In chapter 6, **Jim Cummins** argues the importance of using target language text as input in developing literacy in second/foreign languages. He outlines the theoretical and research bases of technology-supported language learning with reference to his e-Lective Language Learning approach—a departure from traditional methods. Drawing on a decade of research, he emphasizes the merits of Internet- and cd-rom-based scaffolding, as exemplified in online first and second language dictionaries and in learning strategy supports. These are particularly useful for second language learners, who need to catch up with native-speaking peers in minority language learning situations.

Yoko Suzuki and her colleagues provide empirical evidence in chapter 7 about how phonological support, in the form of audio-taped reading models, helps learners to independently increase comprehension and speed of reading. A field test involving nineteen undergraduate, graduate, and research students confirmed that audio supports can help students in three ways; they can present pauses and intonations to facilitate comprehension, present readings of kanji characters, and help students to read faster. The authors also found that students increased their retention of material and improved their concentration.

In chapter 8, **Masako Douglas** critically evaluates Japanese language courses designed for Japanese heritage language learners at the University of California, Los Angeles. Traditionally, these students are fluent in basic interpersonal language skills from home-based exposure but are behind in literacy and formal registers. Regular language programs are designed primarily for JSL students. Now Internet technology provides a "virtual environment" that allows learners to interact with various text materials with a high degree of autonomy. Douglas documents successful curriculum design, use of technology, and assessment of technology-supported individualized instruction in detail, with special focus on reading skills and kanji acquisition.

Chapter 9 (Part IV) discusses copyright issues. **Akifumi Oikawa** is a pioneer in database construction for research in the humanities and is the founding member of the CASTEL/J database research group. He presents a detailed description of how the CASTEL/J database evolved to its current incarnation with seven dictionaries and various full-text databases. He then discusses copyright in Japan and copyright implications for disseminating the CASTEL/J databases as teaching material.

The nine chapters in this volume represent a major effort in Japanese language education to rethink traditional notions and practices. This new direction in research will contribute to improving our understanding of language education in general. We must all prepare ourselves for change, since half the world's population will likely be "wired" by 2020. This book offers a glimpse of what is coming. In this day and age, technological innovations are advancing at such a rapid pace that our story will need "to be continued...."

References

Becker, J.D. 1985. "Typing Chinese, Japanese and Korean." Reprint, *Computer Magazine.*

Jorden, E.H. 2000. "Where Do We Go from Here? And Where Is Here?" Keynote speech at the 12th Annual Conference of the Central Association of Teachers of Japanese, April 14-15, 2000, Washington University in St. Louis.

Kaiho, H., and Y. Nomura. 1983. *Kanji joho shori no shinrigaku* (The Psychology of Kanji Information Processing). Tokyo: Kyoiku Shuppan.

Kaplan, R.B. 1966. "Cultural Thought Patterns in Inter-cultural Education." *Language Learning* 16, no. 1: 1–20.

Suzuki, T. 1978. *Kotoba no ningengaku* (The Humanistic Study of Language). Tokyo: Japan Broadcasting Corporation.

Part One
Language Learning in the Network Society

Using Multimedia in the Network Society

Kanji Akahori

Three recent phases of human society—industrial, information and network—have had a global influence on methods of learning and teaching. This chapter begins with an overview of these developmental phases and their implications for methods of learning and teaching. It then focuses on the network society, addressing two approaches of multimedia learning and their research methods. Within this context the chapter describes several Japanese language systems that my colleagues and I developed using two types of multimedia; first, stand-alone, and second, network-based through the Internet. The chapter closes with a look at issues and prospective future research in developing multimedia materials for JSL (Japanese as a second language) learners.

Media and Society: Three Eras

In order to understand the relationship between media and learning, we must consider a framework of learning theory. Table 1.1 illustrates the relationship among social change, learning media, research methods, and school education (Akahori, 1996).

In an industrial society, the principal goal is to manufacture goods, the objective is efficiency, and the method is the systems approach. The systems approach dissolves an object into parts and recombines these parts to maximize the goal. This approach has entered education as Instructional System Design (Johnson and Foa, 1989). It achieves efficiency by use of audiovisual aids, and programmed instruction as the method of instruction.

In an information society, the goal is to produce information or knowledge. The systems approach, which focuses on input

A

Society	Object	Research Framework	Objectives
Industrial Society	Manufactured goods	Systems approach	Efficiency: outcome-based
Information Society	Knowledge	Information processing model	Knowledge in our brain: process-based
Network Society	Communication	Social interaction	Relationship among humans and society

B

Method	Research Methods	Learning Media	Problems
Resolution to components	Experimental design	Audiovisual/ programmed instruction	Teacher-centered Individual learning Whole class
Structuring	Protocol/learning history analysis	CAI/CAL Hypermedia	Cost performance Curriclum design Teaching strategy
Synthesis	Protocol/ qualitative analysis	Learning environments CSCL* Internet	

* Computer-supported collaborative learning

Table 1.1. Learning media corresponding to society.

and output, is not practical here, because the information society focuses on process. The information-processing model, sometimes called the cognitive approach, works not only for computer science but also for computer-assisted instruction (CAI). The Intelligent Tutoring System (ITS), for example, was developed based on the information-processing or cognitive-process model. Another example, hypermedia learning materials, has been very successful and is widespread in education. These are designed to replicate the metaphor of association in the human brain. Therefore, ITS and hypermedia are founded on the information-processing model, unlike traditional CAI and audiovisual aids.

In the new network society, computer-mediated interaction among humans has become an important goal. Toward this end, researchers focus on how computers or the Internet can assist human interaction, rather than on how a computer can facilitate individual learning. In education, collaborative learning, or GroupWare, has become an attractive research topic. Research in computer-mediated systems often uses qualitative analysis and protocol analysis to investigate social interaction (Kuutti, 1996).

The Internet, the Intranet, and the local area network (LAN) in the classroom and on campus are probably the most representative environments in the network society. Learning media have changed from learning tools, such as audiovisual aids and computer-assisted tools, to learning environments, such as networks and web-based databases. The worldwide web on the Internet contains a wealth of information produced by institutions, professionals, and individuals in various fields. This makes the Internet an important environment which can connect learners to society at large.

To summarize the three eras, in the industrial era, audiovisual aids expanded the reach of the human senses. Audiovisual aids and computer-based programmed instruction maximized learning and enabled society to achieve its core objective, "efficiency" (key word). Audiovisual aids or computer-based drill materials, among other types of learning tools, were common in actual classrooms.

The information society which followed focused on hypermedia and ITS based on the model of "information processing" (key word). Hypermedia-based materials became more widespread in classrooms than ITS because hypermedia structure is less complicated than ITS.

Then in the network era, new programs developed to assist "human interaction" (key word) within society. These include the Internet, computer-supported collaborative learning (CSCL), and the computer-supported intentional learning environment (CSILE). Current web-based learning materials are, however, still very few, especially in Japanese language learning.

Multimedia Materials: Two Approaches

Part B of Table 1.1 describes the relationship between multimedia and learning. If, for example, the multimedia are the platform-integrating multi-modal types of information realized by digital technology, then their materials are based on the human information processing model. If, in contrast, the multimedia consist of the environment represented by the Internet, then their materials are based on social interaction. The key difference is whether or not the multimedia materials involve human interaction. As Computer Supported Collaborative Learning (CSCL) shows in its very title, the key word is "collaboration." This element distinguishes the network-based learning system from the stand-alone system. Currently there are few Japanese language learning systems that are network-based, so I report on both types of materials—stand-alone and network-based.

Stand-alone Japanese Language Learning Materials

Almost all commercial language learning materials are currently on the stand-alone system. In this section, in order to evaluate the effectiveness of the multimedia approach in a stand-alone system, I first compare a new multimedia system with a text-based method, and then show how we harnessed a multimedia approach to a popular Japanese movie.

Assessing Multimedia versus Text

The multimedia system development evolved from a talk with a foreign student, Oh Sofun, who was studying in my laboratory. When she arrived at the Tokyo International Air Terminal from Taiwan, she realized how difficult it was to find and use the train and the bus to travel to her apartment. Foreigners often fear making conversation during transit. She and I surmised that multimedia materials might help reduce such fear (Oh Sofun and Akahori, 1994).

Multimedia on the computer can be effective at "virtually" representing a situation. Although a movie or a video, which uses the analog format, can depict such a scenario realistically for learners to view, multimedia, which uses the digital format, enables learners to interact with the material. This difference, analog or digital, is very important. By interacting within the digital format, learners can construct cognitive models in their brains as they experience the virtual transit situation. They can practise conversations in various situations, buying a ticket, asking for directions, and so on. In order to confirm this assumption, we made a research plan.

We wanted to be able to evaluate the effectiveness of the multimedia material for reducing a learner's fear. However, software evaluation is not easy and takes many forms. Almost all methods of evaluation use subjective questionnaires by comparing two types of material. In our case, experimental subjects could not answer until they had the experience in question, namely, taking transportation between two specific locations. Subjective questionnaires were of little value for assessing our learning materials. Therefore we developed a new evaluation method.

Construction of Material

We prepared two types of materials: multimedia material and text material with almost the same content. The multimedia material deals with how to take a train, a bus, or a taxi, and contains instructions on how to read the bulletin board at the station or bus stop in several modes, such as text, voices, still pictures, and motion pictures. We wrote an instruction manual in Japanese and Chinese. We also videotaped instructional mini-movies, then installed the videos in the computer to create an interactive mode.

Experimental Subjects

Our subjects were eight foreign students at Tokyo Institute of Technology who came from Taiwan within half a year and were not fluent in Japanese. We divided them into two groups, text and multimedia.

Evaluation Method

We measured the time it takes to travel from the university (O-okayama station) to a bus stop at an apartment building near the Akabane station while taking transportation as the map in Figure 1.1 shows. This trip takes about one and a half hours for an experienced resident Japanese. We measured the time it took foreign students in both the text and multimedia groups to reach certain points (Figure 1.2). Figure 1.2 shows the difference. The

Figure 1.1 Route map from university to apartment building.

vertical axis shows the extra time taken by foreign students at certain checkpoints compared to experienced resident Japanese. The horizontal axis shows time taken for the following tasks:

1. from buying a ticket to reaching the platform at O-okayama station
2. travelling from O-okayama station to Meguro station on the Mekama line
3. walking to Yamanote-line platform at Meguro station
4. travelling from Meguro station to Shinjyuku station on the Yamanote line
5. walking to Saikyo-line platform at the Shinjyuku station
6. travelling from Shinjyuku station to Akabane station on the Saikyo line
7. walking to the bus stop in front of the Akabane station
8. reaching the bus stop nearest the apartment building

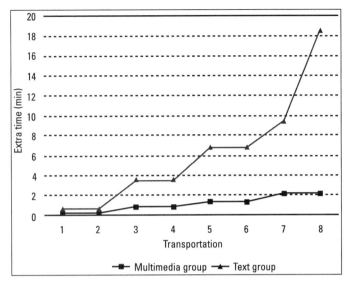

Horizontal axis; checkpoints
Plotted values; average time of four subjects of each group

Figure 1.2 Comparison of time taken by text and by multimedia groups.

Figure 1.2 reveals a clear difference between the text and multimedia groups. Values in Figure 1.2 show the average time taken for each of the four subjects at each checkpoint. Interviews with the subjects of the multimedia group revealed that they felt no fear in taking public transit because the conversation required for buying the ticket and riding was nearly the same as that in the multimedia material. The result shows that our assumption was correct.

Multimedia Material and a Popular Movie

This section describes interactive multimedia language learning material developed on CD-ROM from a popular Japanese movie. The Multimedia Research Project was organized within the Society for Teaching Japanese as a Foreign Language, commissioned by the Agency of Cultural Affairs in the Ministry of Education. I was the project leader. Other members included K. Katoh, S. Nitoguri, I. Saita, and K. Tajima. Details of the project appear in reports on the Committee of Multimedia Research (1997, 1998). Here I provide an overview of the material and some problems we encountered in its development.

Turi-baka Nisshi (The Diary of an Expert Fisherman) is one of the most popular movies produced recently by Shochiku Studio. Our multimedia program consists of three components: the motion picture itself, the entire script of the movie, and a quiz. Students watch part of the motion picture containing a dialogue and click the speech-text button on the screen. Learners can learn how to conduct a conversation corresponding to the situation by watching the motion picture. Screen examples appear in Figure 1.3 and 1.4.

Figure 1.3 shows an example of the quiz in which the learners answer while the help window displays the scene corresponding to the quiz. Figure 1.4 shows the text of the dialogue and its corresponding scene. This system was effective because learners could comprehend the speech better when it was shown together with the scene.

Several practical problems did arise in this project. The most serious one was to obtain permission from Shochiku, the copyright holders, to use the movie, but we succeeded. There are many movies that would work well as multimedia language learning material, but conversion to digital form changes and transfers the original creation, thereby violating copyright. Another issue was that the level of students' and instructor's computer skill varied considerably. Editing the software also proved complex. For example, changing the window size or the motion picture's size in the CD-ROM material was not simple.

Overall, however, this project shows that the use of multimedia is viable for language learning because of its interactivity and its ability to provide context. Interactivity promotes learning by encouraging mutual, active exchange between two agents, the student and the micro-world in the computer. The learner experiences cognitive learning by acting within the virtual environment, the micro-world, of the computer. The student learns by working in the environment rather than by receiving data from it. Context combines particular conversation with its corresponding scene. Many researchers report that contexts facilitate students' understanding of the speech; if they know the situation, they can understand and almost reason out the speaker's intention from non-verbal behavior. Multimedia can offer an appropriate environment for realizing contexts in the computer.

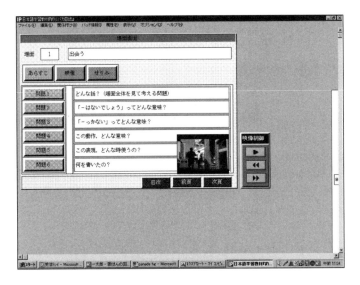

Figure 1.3. Quiz display combined with scene from motion picture.

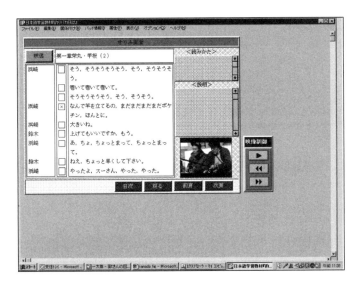

Figure 1.4. Actors' speech display combined with scene from motion picture.

Internet Learning: Three Examples

Recently, the number of language learning systems available on the Internet has been increasing gradually. In this section I look at three network-based Japanese language learning systems that we developed at my laboratory: a system for learning writing on the Internet, a comic-strip database, and a system to help students convert kanji characters to hiragana scripts. Web-based materials contrast with stand-alone types and allow access to the materials anywhere, at any time, and to anyone.

Writing on the Internet

Generally speaking, foreign students inspired by their experiences in Japan are interested in learning the Japanese language. This study started with a foreign student's interest. It is difficult for foreign students, especially those in science and engineering, to attend Japanese classes because they are too busy. Graduate students in any field are also busy, conducting research. As the computer network is spread widely on campuses, foreign students can at any time freely gain access from their laboratory to learning materials stored on the server computer. Under these conditions, Yang and Akahori (1998, 1999) started to develop a computer-assisted language learning (CALL) system based on the web.

Background

Many researchers have reported the effectiveness of the CALL system (Nagata, 1995). Unlike the situation in the classroom, CALL makes it possible to practise freely at any time on the computer. Moreover, the detailed history of a learner's operation can be logged in on the computer. However, learners cannot key in sentences of the target language freely in the current CALL system, particularly in a computer-assisted "writing" system to promote writing skill. They must simply accept the curriculum, which is pre-installed in the computer. Such a system is not interactive.

To overcome this drawback, more and more research is being conducted using natural language processing (NLP) techniques in the CALL system (Yamamoto et al., 1996; Yang and Akahori, 1998,

1999). This enables students on the CALL system to phrase and type in their own sentences freely, without following set rules. Research on error analysis (Juozulynas, 1994; Nagata, 1995) has improved significantly since excellent experimental results in the robustness of NLP were achieved. Unfortunately, almost all the grammar theories and techniques of NLP proposed until now can analyze only grammatically correct sentences. Language learners who use the CALL system are more likely to key in ill-formed sentences. Thus, we must either add an error analyzer to the current uncertified NLP tools or rectify NLP tools to correct this problem.

As for computer analysis of the Japanese language, it is difficult to determine the correct morpheme (or part of speech), even in a grammatically correct sentence, because the sentence in Japanese is written continuously, without any spaces. A simple example is "Jirou was hit by Tarou." The expression of Japanese in romaji (Roman letters) is written with spaces between words. Recasting the above example, we read "Jirou wa Tarou ni naguraremashita." Thus, because of the continuity of characters in Japanese, currently available NLP tools will interpret an ill-formed sentence as grammatically correct and obtain the incorrect morpheme. For example, the correct sentence with the correct morpheme "Jirou | wa | Tarou | ni | nagura | re | mashita" will be analyzed as "Jirou | wa | Tarou | nina | kura | re | mashita," when the correct word "naguraremashita (be hit)" is typed as the incorrect word "nakuraremashita."

For this reason, there are very few systems for teaching writing in Japanese using NLP techniques. Nihongo-CALI (Japanese Computer-Assisted Language Instruction) uses NLP tools to analyze the learner's typed sentence and to generate feedback (Nagata, 1995), but it accepts the expression of Japanese sentences only in *romaji*, not in kana and kanji. In our present system, learners can key in Japanese sentences in kana and kanji and obtain the correct morpheme even from an ill-formed sentence.

Matsumoto and Imaichi (1994) proposed some approaches for parsing ill-formed input. Together with J.C. Yang, a graduate student in my laboratory, I conducted a study in which we used a similar approach, predicting the structure of ill-formed input and then writing it into the system for the purpose of error analysis (Yang and Akahori, 1998, 1999). In our approach, the first step was to identify the structure of possibly erroneous sentences in passive voice, and then form rules to decide the correctness of sentences.

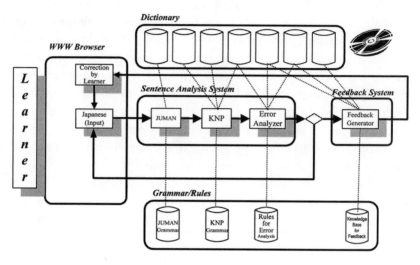

Figure 1.5. Diagram of the CALL System

By implementing these NLP techniques in the CALL system, we improved the system's methods of error analysis. The learner can key in sentences freely on any web browser and will receive feedback on errors detected by the system.

The CALL System using NLP

The CALL system using NLP, as illustrated in the diagram (Figure 1.5), consists of five components: Web Browser, Sentence Analysis System, Feedback System, Dictionary, and Grammar/Rules. The Sentence Analysis System has analyzers for morphemes, syntax, and errors. The present system analyzes a typed Japanese sentence, first in the morpheme analyzer, second in the syntax analyzer, and finally in the error analyzer. Rules-for-Error Analysis detects the type of error (that is, Error ID). The feedback system includes a Feedback Messages Generator, a Knowledge Database for Feedback, and a list of all learning histories during the operation of the system. Adequate feedback messages go to the learner, according to the type of error and relative information received as output from sentence analysis.

Registration, which includes the learner's name and level of experience of Japanese learning, must precede use of this system and provides feedback and analysis of the student's learning situation. The student operates this system according to instructions written on the web page. The initial page consists of several pictures from which the student can select a topic. When the student chooses one of them, a large picture of the selected icon and a text box appear on a new page. The student can key in the Japanese sentence written in the passive voice, for example, in the text box under the visual, then type the text in both kana and kanji, the usual input method of most Japanese word processors. The system gives feedback if it detects any errors, and requires the learner to make corrections by repeating all the steps. Figure 1.6 illustrates the initial page where the learner keys in the sentence; Figure 1.7 shows feedback about the wrong conjugation of the verb in passive voice.

In order to evaluate the adequacy of this system, we included a questionnaire page for the users. Figure 1.8 shows part of the questionnaire on the web. Within one and a half years, we received over ten thousand responses from viewers all over the world, and almost all comments were favourable and encouraging. This means that Japanese learners all over the world appreciate web-based language materials being accessible at any time and from anywhere.

A Comic-Strip Database

This material was developed by a research project sponsored by the Research Institute of the Software Engineering Foundation (Research Committee, 1998; Akahori et al., 1998). I was the project leader.

System Design

This system has a database containing one hundred comic strips. Dialogues appear both in Japanese and in English. Each comic strip consists of four frames that illustrate everyday situations. Japanese expressions become easier for learners to understand when presented in appropriate situations. Motion pictures are preferable, but they are hard to adapt to web-based materials because of the huge memory and access time required. These four-frame strips are quickly accessible through the Internet and learners can readily recognize the situation.

A retrieval system was implemented to help learners understand how a word is used in various situations. For example, "you" is expressed by various Japanese words, such as "anata," "kimi," and

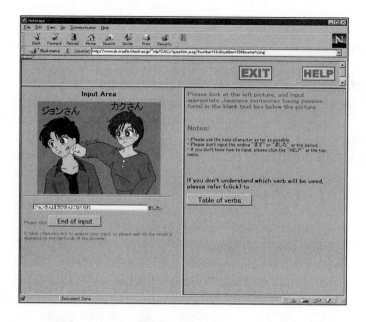

Figure 1.6. The initial page of the CALL System

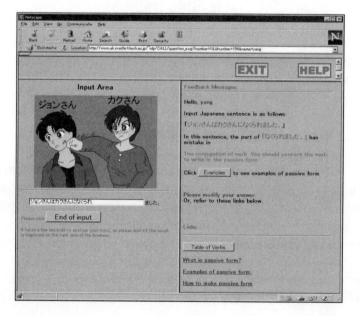

Figure 1.7. Feedback messages regarding incorrect use of the verb in passive voice.

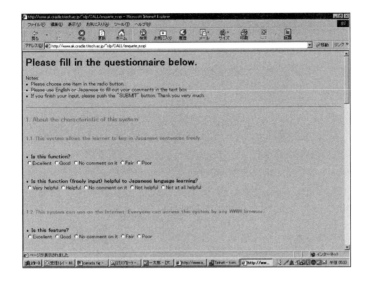

Figure 1.8. Questionnaire on the web for the CALL System.

"omae," which are situation-dependent. By searching how to employ a word in various situations, learners can learn to use it correctly.

Audio or "voices" form an important part of the system. Professional voice actors speak for the characters in the comic story, recorded into the computer.

Because of the problem of copyright, we could not use commercial comic stories that are published in magazines and other books. In order to create a database, we had an expert comic artist produce a hundred comic stories.

System Development

Learners can reach the comic-story database through a web browser. The system consists of two main modules: a database and a retrieval module. The retrieval system is based on two methods, free keyword input and menu selection.

Learners can choose three retrieval methods. "Words and phrases" is a free keyword method; "titles" means selection of comic story titles arranged in alphabetical order; and "situation" is a method of menu selection presenting various categories such as seasons, everyday life, and cultural issues.

We prepared two types of display. In one type, the frames appear successively, according to the story's expansion. When the learner pushes the voice button, the first frame appears along with the sounds of the characters' voices, then the next frame, and so on. The other type offers a simultaneous display of all four frames. The characters' words and the related words, with the topics, are explained in English on another window, so that non-Japanese students can understand the meaning.

When learners finish interacting with the learning system, questions are displayed, and answers are recorded automatically in the files, together with the learning history stored in the server computer.

Figure 1.9 shows an example of the free keyword input-retrieval display, where a learner can input the word in Japanese or in English. In this picture, the input word is "you," and the comic stories in which characters' words contain "you" are displayed. Figure 1.10 shows an example of a retrieved display.

Figure 1.11 shows an example of successive display, with the first frame displayed here. This method permits the display of each frame coinciding with actual speech. Figure 1.12 shows the fourth frame, an example of a comic story. Figure 1.13 shows commentary in English, whereby a learner can grasp the meaning of the characters' words and the accompanying, background Japanese culture.

Evaluation

Twenty-four Japanese instructors answered a questionnaire about the system. Their observations included the following:

- Inclusion of actual speech in the system was very effective in language learning.
- The context-based system of language learning was especially effective in motivating learners. Delivery of materials to instructors through the web was excellent.
- Clarification of copyright issues is important for implementation of web-based learning systems.

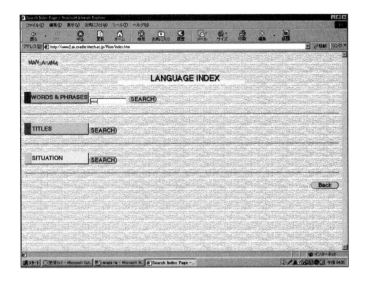

Figure 1.9. Retrieval display of a comic database.

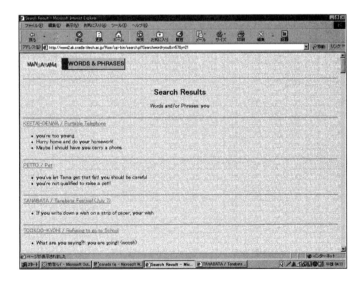

Figure 1.10. Example of a comic story retrieved by a keyword.

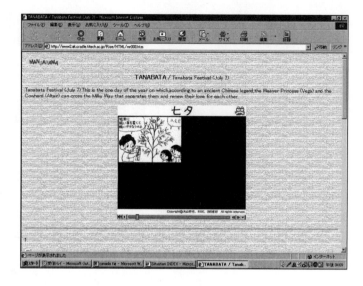

Figure 1.11. Display of the first frame of a comic story.

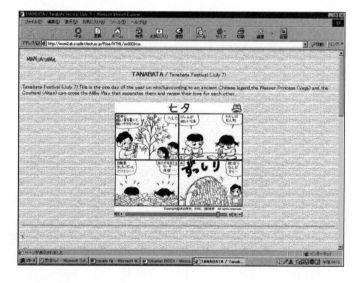

Figure 1.12. Example of a comic story.

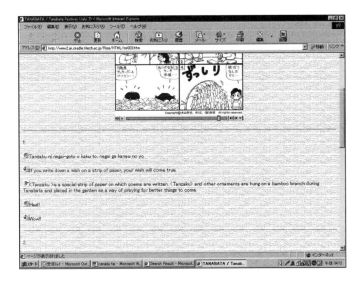

Figure 1.13. Commentary in English of the dialogue.

The Comic-strip Database Study was conducted by the project team, which included N. Furugohri, K. Katoh, A. Nitoguri, S. Usami, and T. Yoshioka. The material can be accessed at <http://www2.ak.cradle.titech.ac.jp/Rise/top.htm>.

Changing Kanji to Hiragana

My student S. Fujitani, and I designed a help system (Fujitani, and Akahori, 1999a, 1999b) to be used by children of Japanese schools outside of Japan. It contains a mailing list so that teachers and students in Japanese schools can collaborate internationally.

Not only foreigners but also native Japanese children find it difficult to learn Japanese, especially kanji characters. Young children in elementary school cannot read and write complex kanji characters. Yet it is also difficult for them to read sentences all written in hiragana, because they are familiar with reading sentences with kanji and hiragana together. On our help system, when a learner touches the kanji with the mouse cursor, our tool displays hiragana right beside the kanji. This tool might also be useful for JSL learners. Its URL address is http://www.ak.cradle.titech.ac.jp/ngp/index.shml.

Figure 1.14 shows the home page of the project. We have been managing and organizing the project on a volunteer basis since 1996. Members number over 330, and almost all Japanese schools outside of Japan are involved. They have conducted many learning activities, such as collaborative learning, information exchanges, counselling, and questions and answers.

Figure 1.15 shows an example of the display of hiragana. We developed this help tool by applying NLP techniques. At first, a morpheme analyzer in the server dissolves a sentence into words. Next, another program selects kanji by matching these separated words with a dictionary on the server, picking up the corresponding hiragana and displaying it. Figure 1.15 shows the word "okonawareru" displayed in hiragana.

Problems and Future Research

Development of Internet-based Japanese Language Materials

The Internet is the most effective environment for developing Internet-based Japanese language materials, especially for Japanese language instructors outside of Japan, because it is difficult otherwise to obtain suitable and free materials. Videotapes and textbooks are expensive. Through the Internet, teachers can obtain useful materials at any time from anywhere.

Use of a Variety of Media

It is difficult to view motion pictures through the Internet because of the time and speed required. Video is more convenient than the Internet, but it is expensive and non-interactive. Therefore, it is practical for instructors to combine a variety of media, such as textbooks, video, computers, and the Internet, according to the learning situation and instructional strategy.

Provision of Easy-to-Customize Materials

Instructors sometimes want to adjust materials for their students according to the students' interest, specialized fields, and proficiency levels, and also according to the class size. When instructors acquire

Figure 1.14. Home page of the overseas Japanese schools project.

Figure 1.15. Example of a hiragana display.

materials through the Internet or CD-ROM, ideally they should be able to customize them easily, but current authoring tools are difficult for instructors to operate.

Links to Useful Japanese Language Learning Web Pages

Many institutions and individuals have been producing home pages for learning Japanese. A truly integrated home page will contain a portal site that collects all information on and provides links to sites committed to effective Japanese language learning. The establishment of such portal sites is essential for promoting foreign language education.

Conclusions

The network society offers extraordinary possibilities for assisting those seeking to learn the Japanese language. The two stand-alone multimedia systems and the three Internet-based systems analyzed above show great potential yet pose attendant problems in copyright, expense, and difficulty of adaptation. Nonetheless, especially outside Japan, these systems are transforming the process of learning Japanese and offer opportunities undreamed of until now.

References

Akahori, K. 1996. "Some Features and Problems of Research Methodology in Educational Technology." *Proceedings of the 12th Annual Conference of Japan Society of Educational Technology*, 133–4.

Akahori, K., T. Yoshioka, S. Usami, K. Katoh, and A. Nitoguri. 1998. "Web-based Japanese Learning Materials Constructed by Comic Story Database." *Proceedings of Conference on Education Technology in Japan*, 545–6.

Arai, K., and K. Akahori. 1998. "Development of Japanese Learning System Based on Comic Stories Applying Natural Language Technique." *Research Report of Electronic Information & Communication Society in Japan*, ET98–36, 39–46.

Committee of Multimedia Research in Japan Society of Japanese Education. 1997. *Research Report on Multimedia Japanese Language Learning Materials in 1997.* Japan Society of Japanese Language Education and Agency of Cultural Affairs in the Ministry of Education.

Committee of Multimedia Research in Japan Society of Japanese Education. 1998. *Research Report on Multimedia Japanese Language Learning Materials in 1998.* Japan Society of Japanese Language Education and Agency of Cultural Affairs in the Ministry of Education.

Fujitani, S., and K, Akahori. 1999a. "A Practical Study on Management and Support of Japanese School Overseas Project." *Journal of Educational System and Information Society in Japan* 16, no. 1: 13–21.

Fujitani, S., and K, Akahori. 1999b. "A Summary Sentence Extraction Method for Web-Based Mailing List Review: Application and Its Effectiveness Study." *Advanced Research in Computer and Communications in Education* 1: 327–34.

Hannafin, M.J., and S.M. Land. 1997. "The Foundations and Assumptions of Technology Enhanced Student Centered Learning Environments." *Instructional Science* 22, no. 3: 167–202.

Johnson, K.A., and L.J. Foa. 1989. *Instructional Design.* National University Continuing Education Association (NUCEA). New York: Macmillan.

Juozulynas, V. 1994. "Errors in the Compositions of Second-Year German Students: An Empirical Study for Parser-Based ICALI." *CALICO Journal* 12, no. 1: 5–15.

Kuutti, K. 1996. "Active Theory as a Potential Framework for Human Computer Interaction." In Bonnie A. Nardi, ed., *Context and Consciousness,* 17–44. Cambridge, Mass.: MIT Press.

Matsumoto, Y., and O. Imaichi. 1994. "Current Issues in Robust Natural Language Processing." (in Japanese) In *Proceedings of the First SIG-SLP Conference of the Information Processing Society of Japan.*

Nagao, M. 1996. *Natural Language Processing* (in Japanese). Tokyo: Iwanami Syoten.

Nagata, N. 1995. An Effective Application of Natural Language Processing in Second Language Instruction." *CALICO Journal* 13, no. 1: 47–67.

Oh Sofun, and K. Akahori. 1994. "Development and Evaluation of Multimedia Japanese Language Learning System for Chinese." *Research Report of JET (Japan Educational Technology) Conference,* 94–2, 117–20.

Research Committee in Research Institute of Software Engineering Foundation. 1997. *A Survey Report on Japanese Language Learning Materials in Foreign Countries* (in Japanese). Research Institute of Software Engineering Foundation.

Research Committee in Research Institute of Software Engineering Foundation. 1998. *A Report on Development of Japanese Language Learning System Based on Comic Stories* (in Japanese). Research Institute of Software Engineering Foundation.

Yamamoto, H., M. Sakayauchi, and R. Yoshioka. 1996. "Development of the System of Japanese Teaching Material Using CASTEL/J." In *Proceedings of the 20th Annual Conference of the Japan Society for Science Education* (in Japanese), 105–6.

Yang, J.C., and K. Akahori. 1998. "Error Analysis in Japanese Writing and Its Implementation in a Computer Assisted Language Learning System on the World Wide Web. *CALICO Journal* 15, 47–66.

Yang, J.C., and K. Akahori. 1999. "An Evaluation of Japanese call System on the www Comparing a Freely Input Approach with Multiple Selection." *CALL (Computer Assisted Language Learning) Journal* 12, no. 1: 59–79.

Developing CALL Software

Michio Tsutsui

Introduction

Rapid advances in technology in recent years have transformed the environment for computer use in foreign language education. Computing facilities at academic institutions are continually being updated and improved, and many people have personal computers at home; the Internet and e-mail have become common tools for both teachers and students. Technological advances in multimedia, digital sound/video recording and processing, mass storage media (gigabit magnetic disc drives and various optical disc devices), and natural language processing (character recognition, voice recognition, voice synthesis, and machine translation) offer a number of attractive tools for language education (see Figure 2.1). Furthermore, recent Windows and Macintosh operating systems provide foreign-language support as a standard feature.

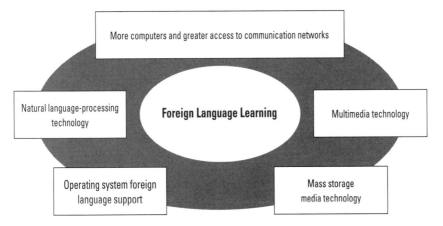

Figure 2.1. Changes to the technical environment of foreign language learning.

Many projects are currently being launched in technology-enhanced language learning, but it is necessary to proceed carefully. Mistakes in directing projects may produce results which are not as fruitful as we expect. Of the many software development projects in CALL, few have benefited a wide base of users, had a long life, or further advanced CALL.

Why is this the case? To answer this, we must look at different stages of product development. In the main body of this chapter, I focus on four common problem areas: technology assessment, software design, dissemination, and collaboration. I discuss these issues based on my experience with the development of CALL software at the University of Washington, in the hope that future CALL projects can yield more usable products and that those products can benefit a broader base of users. First, however, I give a brief overview of the CALL program Language Partner, which provides the background for the discussion below.

Overview of Language Partner

Language Partner is an interactive multimedia program that we developed at the University of Washington to assist students in acquiring oral communication skills effectively with minimum effort. It enables students to prepare for conversation classes so that they can spend classroom hours in more advanced practice such as dialogue expansion and application for real situations.[1] The program was initially called Nihongo Partner and was originally developed specifically for Japanese language education. However, the current version can be used with any language as long as the computer platform supports that language.

Using the most recent multimedia technologies, Language Partner creates a practice environment that simulates real situations so that learners can feel as if they have real conversation partners when they practice dialogues. Because the program uses video, learners can acquire simultaneously not only verbal but also nonverbal skills, such as body movements and facial expressions. The program's step-by-step approach, together with other functions, allows students to learn dialogues almost effortlessly.

The accompanying authoring tool enables instructors to create their own video dialogue materials to run on Language Partner without special resources or technical expertise.

Language Partner provides learners with a simple and easy-to-use interface consisting of three sessions: preview, repeat-after-me, and interaction. First, in the preview session (Figure 2.2), learners view a given dialogue from a third person's point of view and understand its linguistic and cultural content. Second, in the repeat-after-me session (Figure 2.3), learners practice each speaker's lines by repeating after the speakers on the screen. Finally, in the interaction session, learners practice interacting with the speakers on the screen.

To help learners practice dialogues effectively and efficiently, Language Partner provides a number of functions. For example, in the preview session learners can view part of a dialogue repeatedly with a single mouse click. They can, on demand, see dialogue texts and their translations in any session; and, through simple operations, they can record their voices and compare them with the models in the repeat-after-me and interaction sessions. Language Partner is designed on the assumption that instructors will develop video materials for the program according to their educational objectives, available resources and so on. They can create video materials using the accompanying authoring tool, LP Author, and a video camera. The materials are stored in the database, LP Library, and they are maintained using the accompanying utility program, LP Database Tool. (Figure 2.4)

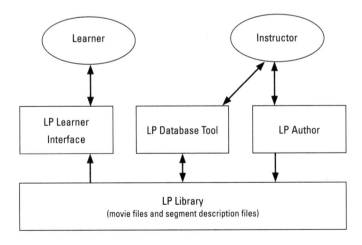

Figure 2.4. Language Partner overview.

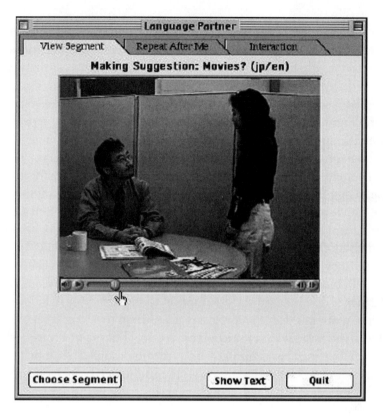

Figure 2.2. Language Partner's preview session.

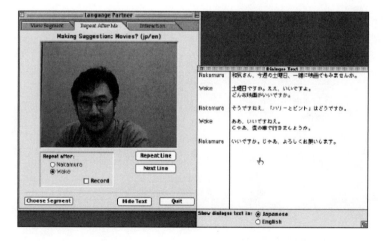

Figure 2.3. Language Partner's repeat-after-me session.

Language Partner's video materials are all digitized data and can be stored in mass storage medium such as local hard discs, servers, and various optical storage media. Thus the program can be used either locally or remotely. In addition, it is easy to exchange developed materials between institutions, to keep materials at one place as a common library to share among several institutions, and to distribute materials widely and in quantity using CD-ROMs. Furthermore, platform changes and software upgrades do not affect Language Partner; therefore, accumulated materials can be used on future systems (Tsutsui et al., 1998a, 1998b).

In the remainder of this chapter, I discuss several issues that I consider central to successful CALL software development: technology assessment, basic design, dissemination, and collaboration.

Technology Assessment

In CALL software development, as in any other technology development, it is important to assess available technologies before beginning a specific design. This step is critical because of the rapid pace and complexity of technology development. Failure to undertake careful assessment may put projects in jeopardy later. For example, a technology selected for a software development project may not exhibit the expected performance, such as adequate processing speed or stable performance, or may not perform a critical function properly, such as the recording function or language support. Occasionally, the developer of the selected technology may discontinue its development or the company may shut down. Release of a new technology under development sometimes makes a chosen technology obsolete. Such situations are not uncommon and may not be entirely avoidable. Careful assessment will certainly reduce such risks.

It is clear from the above examples that, when deciding what specific hardware and/or software technology to adopt in developing an intended software program, knowing merely what technology satisfies the product's technical needs or which software/hardware product gives the best performance may not be enough. Equally important questions may be:

- How stable is the technology under assessment?
- How much does it cost?
- How widely is it used?
- How promising is it?
- In what direction will it develop?
- Will there soon be a superseding technology? And, if so, when?
- If there is a problem that no current technology can solve, how likely is it that a new technology will solve it?
- If there is more than one technology to choose from, which will become the standard technology?
- How fast will the related infrastructure expand locally or globally?

Obviously, many of these issues are beyond the knowledge of most language instructors. Thus, during technology assessment, it is essential to involve technical specialists with good perspective and insight. In many earlier CALL projects, the project teams did not involve such specialists.

In assessing available technologies, one must also examine carefully the operational feasibility of the technology. For example, even when a given technology has the capability to prevent the development of a powerful software program, that technology will be appropriate only if the supporting infrastructure, staff, and so forth, are equipped to handle it.

Software Design

Several design-related issues require serious consideration if CALL development is to lead to software that can attract a large body of users. Here I focus on two, usability and expandability/flexibility, because these issues have not received enough attention in the CALL community. This oversight may help explain the scarcity of software that can be used by a broader population.[2]

Usability

"Usability" is a key word in product design today. For both hardware and software, high performance and attractive functions are not enough; a product must be designed and made so that it can be used with a minimum of effort. CALL software is no exception. Ease of use is a concern both in the learning stage and in the operation stage where the operations are often routine.[3] The factors affecting usability differ in the two stages. The software industry has developed a number of new concepts and approaches to improve usability in both stages. For example, on-line tutorials facilitate learning, and split windows and undo/redo commands increase operational usability. Navigation systems and on-line help are intended to achieve high usability in both stages.

For CALL software, the learning stage is relatively easy. It is operational usability that requires the most attention. The following are seven checkpoints to improve operational usability:

- *Simplicity*: Operations must be simple, requiring only a click of a mouse or a stroke of a key, and no task should require more than a minimal number of steps.
- *Naturalness*: Operations should accord with natural hand and eye movement.
- *Directness*: Operations must require a minimum amount of thought. There should be no confusing messages, buttons, and so on.
- *Spontaneity*: Operations should rely on intuition/common sense, using familiar symbols, colours, etc.
- *Flexibility*: Operations must be flexible for ease of use, providing, for example, multiple paths to go to a certain page.
- *Mistake-free operation*: Chances for "mis-operations" must be minimized. For example, unnecessary buttons should not be displayed.
- *Recoverability*: Ways should be provided to recover from "mis-operations" without having to restart the program.

The educational effectiveness of a software product resides partly in its usability. If a program is difficult to learn and/or operate, more time is required for its use, the possibility of errors increases, and learners may lose their focus and become discouraged. Such products will not be marketable. Thus, CALL software devlopers must pay serious attention to usability. To this end, it is crucial to seek specialists' opinions and to test usability at critical stages in the development process. This is as essential as developing a bug-free product.[4]

In Language Partner, usability has always been a central concern for the development team. Our efforts to ensure usability by obtaining opinions from specialists in foreign language, in computer technology, and in usability, and by testing usability with the help of both student subjects (for the learner interface) and instructor subjects (for the authoring tool) have resulted in a highly refined learner interface and an easy-to-use authoring tool.

To be specific, the latest issue of Language Partner allows the learner to move from one practice session to another freely and smoothly (that is, easy navigation). When learners want to record their voices with the recording and playback functions, the computer automatically switches to the recording mode after the model speaker has spoken a given line; when recording is over, playback begins instantly with a single mouse click (that is, simple and minimal operations). Further, the learner interface displays no unnecessary buttons on the screen in any session, which precludes possible confusion or faulty operations (that is, minimum thinking and mistake-free operations). Both students and instructors greatly appreciate these improvements and the program has attracted many users.

Expandability and Flexibility

Expandability and flexibility are two closely related issues in the design of CALL software. A common problem is that many CALL programs are released as complete products. Such products do not allow users to add new materials (no expandability) or modify the content and/or structure of the materials provided (no flexibility). In contrast to such "closed" programs, open-ended programs allow for addition and/or modification.

Although closed programs may be easier to develop and market than open-ended programs, they have at least three serious disadvantages. First, new materials cannot be added. If instructors want to teach materials that are not in a program, they must use different approaches to teach those materials or give them up. This may cause some inconsistency in class activities, lab assignments, and homework. Second, the materials provided with the program cannot be modified. Suppose, for example, that a program contains some untaught vocabulary items or Chinese characters in its exercises or example sentences. If the program does not allow for modification, the instructor may have to prepare supplementary teaching materials or instruct the students to skip those exercises. Either situation creates frustration for both instructors and students. Third, the structure provided cannot be altered. For example, if an instructor finds the lesson or exercise sequence of the program inappropriate for a set of students, a closed program does not allow for modification. Therefore the instructor must either follow the inappropriate sequence or instruct students to follow a different sequence.

Thus, closed programs frequently cannot meet the users' individual needs and often force instructors to make adjustments. Even if instructors find most features of a program attractive and useful, they may hesitate to use it; or, if they decide to use part of the program, it may not work as effectively as the developers intended.

Although closed programs are typically seen in "read-only media" products such as laser discs and CD-ROMs, non-expandability and inflexibility are the result of a program's design and not the medium itself. Even a program that is potentially expandable and flexible with the use of a "writable" or "rewritable" medium can become a closed program if the user interface and the content are tightly integrated. If CALL software is to benefit a wide range of users, expandability and flexibility must be primary design concerns.

In designing Language Partner, two of our basic objectives were high expandability and flexibility. To this end, we put the teaching materials in the LP Library, completely separate from the Learner Interface (Figure 2.4). Adding new materials or changing existing ones does not affect the program's functionality, as long as internal data formats remain unchanged. In addition, the library's capacity is virtually limitless because users have storage media choices. Materials that need to be on-line can stay in resident storage media, but others can be kept in other media, such as optical discs.

Other design features increase flexibility, for example, the lesson menu system. In Language Partner, dialogue materials are usually a mixture of user-developed materials, shareware, and commercial-ware that reside in one or more physical storage devices. When instructors set up Language Partner, they select the dialogues they want their students to practice from a whole body of existing dialogue materials and register them into the menu in the order in which they want the materials used. Thus, instructors have full control over the selection of materials and their presentation sequence. If they cannot find appropriate dialogues, they can create their own to add to the library.

Dissemination

Another critical aspect of software development is dissemination. Without effective effort in this area, even excellent software will not be widely used. Promotion is a vital part of dissemination. Software projects are commonly promoted through conference presentations, workshops, journal articles, promotional brochures, demo CDs, and promotional web sites. Such promotional activities are essential for CALL projects. Here, I discuss this issue using Language Partner as an interesting model for software dissemination.

As I mentioned above, Language Partner provides a number of features, including dialogue practice using video, step-by-step practice, on-demand presentation of dialogue text and translation, instant recording and playback, open-ended structure, and an easy-to-use authoring tool. However, what makes it fundamentally different from other CALL software is its design, which assumes participation by the user (that is, instructor) in an ongoing development process. In other words, it is not Language Partner's intention to provide a comprehensive or large video dialogue library as part of its program. Instead, it offers both a tool with which instructors can develop their own video dialogues and the "shell" through which they can present those video dialogues for effective practice in oral communication.

The rationale for this approach is the following. First, because educational needs vary, it is impossible to create a set of materials that will satisfy all potential users. It is also difficult for a small development team to create a vast set of materials to satisfy many users. Thus it makes more sense to have users create materials according to their own needs. As stated above, Language Partner encourages such development with its open-ended program design whereby users can add new materials freely and modify existing materials easily. The capacity of the library, with its video dialogues, is virtually limitless, and any mass storage devices can be used.

This user participation software development model offers at least six advantages. First, developers and users can share the development load, reducing the risk that developers will be overburdened. Second, developers and users can concentrate on specific areas of software development (that is, developers can focus on frameworks and tools, and users on content), thus making the best use of their respective resources and expertise. Third, users can add materials and modify existing materials as they like, creating the most suitable materials with minimum effort. Fourth, users can collaborate in developing materials and can share their materials with others, thereby reducing their own development effort. Fifth, if the number of users grows, the collective library will expand, which will attract more users. Thus, if software is successfully disseminated, the materials library will grow along with the body of users. Sixth, the private sector can also participate in materials development, further expanding the library.

In this user-participation model, the number of users in part determines the value of the software, hence the richness of the library. Therefore, effective dissemination is extremely important in this model.

Collaboration

I noted above the value of involving technical specialists in technology assessment and in the development of user interfaces. I also presented a model of CALL software development that involves users in the development of content. Such collaborative efforts, I feel, are vital in ensuring the broad-based success of a software project.

Today's technology is not just complex, it also changes quickly. To keep up with advances takes a lot of time. However, language instructors are usually busy with teaching and other duties and have little time to keep abreast of new technologies, to engage themselves in actual software development, or to maintain developed systems. Although they commonly hire student assistants to alleviate their workload, assistants usually cannot carry heavy responsibility and may not be able to stay with a project as long as needed. Thus, a substantial software development project may not be realistic with such limited personnel.

One possible solution may be collaboration, for example, with specialists in other disciplines (such as computer, educational, and information technologies) or with other institutions, as in the user-participation model that I presented here.

As for collaboration, there are three points to keep in mind. First, specialists in other disciplines may have different interests, concerns, and goals. For example, language instructors may want to develop workable programs, while other specialists may seek only prototypes. Thus, in collaborative effort it is critical to define a project's goals clearly from the start.

Second, the focus of the software project is important. For language instructors, CALL software should be pedagogically sound and educationally effective; sophisticated functions and aesthetic appearance are not significant. In other words, a CALL program with little educational merit is of no use even if it is loaded with advanced technologies.

Finally, in order to encourage collaboration and minimize duplication, developers should have some way to exchange information efficiently about ongoing CALL projects. Setting up a Web bulletin board would serve this purpose.

Conclusion

Today's technical environment is highly inviting for those interested in technology-enhanced language learning, and therefore we may expect many CALL projects to appear. However, if people simply follow conventional development practices, fruitful results are unlikely. In order to develop products that can assist a wide base of users over a period of time, we must re-examine our current approaches to technology assessment, software design, dissemination, and collaboration, so that learners and instructors can take the best advantage of their rich technical environment.

Notes

1. More information on Language Partner is available at the Technical Japanese Program Language Partner page http://www.tjp.washington.edu/lp. The Language Partner demo can be downloaded from this page and can be used for up to six months at no cost. If you are interested in purchasing Language Partner, information is available at the University of Washington Software and Copyright Ventures Language Partner page http://depts.washington.edu/ventures/collabtr/direct/langpart.htm. Questions can be sent via e-mail to lp@tjp.washington.edu.
2. In addition to the issues of usability and expandability/flexibility, the University of Washington development team is also attempting to increase the program's universality in terms of languages and computer platforms. The current version is language-independent; the team is now developing a platform-independent version.
3. In general, the learning stage continues into the second or operational stage, since the user continues learning about the product (for example, new functions, better ways of using it) while using it for production.
4. Dumas and Redish (1999) provide a comprehensive guide to usability, usability methods and techniques, usability testing, and employing test results to improve products.

References

Dumas, J.S., and C. Redish. *A Practical Guide to Usability Testing.* Norwood, NJ: Ablex Publishing. 1993. (Revised paperback edition (1999) available from Intellect Publishing.)

Tsutsui, M., M. Kato, and B. Mohr. 1998a. "Closing the Gap between Practice Environments and Reality: An Interactive Multimedia Program for Oral Communication Training in Japanese (Part 1. Theory)." *Computer Assisted Language Learning: An International Journal* 11, no. 2: 125–38.

Tsutsui, M., M. Kato, and B. Mohr. 1998b. "Closing the Gap between Practice Environments and Reality: An Interactive Multimedia Program for Oral Communication Training in Japanese (Part 2. Practice)." *Computer Assisted Language Learning: An International Journal* 11, no. 2: 138–51.

Part Two
Database-supported Language Education

A Gradual Approach to Technology-Based Instruction

Hilofumi Yamamoto

In this chapter, I discuss the client-server system for language instruction in terms of its use as a computer-managed instruction system (CMI).

Within a client-server system, the client is a computer that receives information from a source computer designated as the server. Information can be passed from the server to the client on a local network or via the Internet. The client-server system discussed in this chapter is generally used on the Internet.

CMI was originally designed for individually prescribed instruction in the 1960s (Glaser, 1967; Lindvall and Bolvin, 1967). It has inspired much research and many practical reports and projects, most notably the PLAN project (Brudner, 1968). It is now used in many fields of education, including vocational education, and on-the-job training, as well as language instruction.

CMI is especially useful for language education. A CMI system can, for example, retrieve students' response data, compute them, generate feedback for each student, and send a summary report to the instructor by e-mail. Instructors can in turn use these e-mail reports to evaluate students' learning profiles and to monitor their ongoing performance. Figures 3.1 and 3.2 describes the use of the computer as a tool for the teacher, and as a self-tutorial tool for the student's language learning.

Language teachers who base their instruction in computer applications must, in addition to teaching the language itself, develop a curriculum and instructional materials from a computer database and calculate students' test and quiz scores with computer aids to

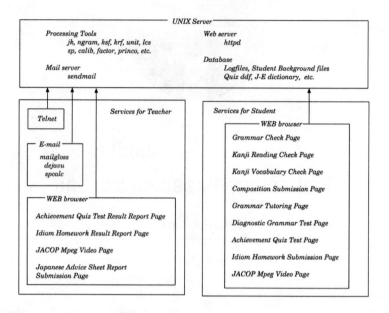

Figure 3.1. Model of client-server system services.

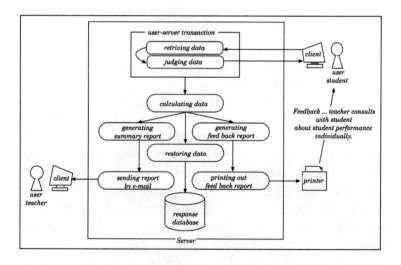

Figure 3.2. Automatic processing of client-server system for language instruction.

assess student progress. In this chapter, I address each of these issues in turn, using a series of theoretical formulae to help explain the process.

Where appropriate, I describe the following specific instructional tools and elaborate on the relationship between the tools and the curriculum: tools for instructors (Unix-based JKWIC and N-gram; Mialgloss and DejaVu on e-mail), and assessment and self-tutorial tools (Diagnostic Grammar Test; Grammar Tutoring System; Grammar Check System; Kanji teaching program).

I have attached a list of these programs and relevant database projects as an appendix.

Methods

The Basic Idea

To explain the development of a system for language instruction, I present an equation containing three variables:

$$L = T - I, \tag{1}$$

where L is a list that the student will learn, T is a list of objectives, including what students should do, and I is a list of what students are able to do now.

In order to enhance T, the instruction designer should describe the teaching syllabus in detail and prepare documents or a database concerning use of the target language, that is, recordings or transcripts of conversation.

To increase the accuracy of I, the designer has to develop valid and reliable tests. At the same time, the system should record students' achievement in detail. This chapter emphasizes equation (1). However, once we have clarified L by calculations, we can decide on the order of the teaching items: which elements $L = \{l, l, l, ...l\}$ to teach first, which second, and so on. Equation (2) can calculate this order. Thus, for the first time, the method (M) will be determined properly:

$$M = f(L). \tag{2}$$

In order to develop robust methods, we subtract what the student can do (I) from the objectives (T). Even if a teacher does not have a professional technique of managing information, he or she can begin computer-managed instruction (CMI) by listing teaching items with spreadsheet software. Ishii (1992) demonstrates this method for Japanese linguistic research and proposes computer use without programming. Whether teachers use a computer or not, they still have to continue thinking of these simple ideas for curriculum development.

The client-server system supports teaching quality in pedagogy and controls spending for hardware and for its management. It is not, however, an all-purpose solution for educational problems. Change to a technology-based system should proceed only gradually.

It is necessary to determine each value in our equations by flexible and practical methods. As mentioned above, the test must have high reliability and validity. How do we develop such a test? Of course, it is impossible to do so overnight. We need a considered and practical development plan for tests and materials. We need to improve test values gradually, and the calculation of L must be sufficiently accurate.

In the following subsections, I introduce the databases to clarify T, the tools for material development to calculate L, and also web applications to ascertain students' language knowledge—I.

Use of Databases

What is variable T? In other words, what is in the text that will be taught? It is quite easy to determine that with a database (Ogino, 1981; Takefuta, 1986; Nakano, 1996). When teachers use a database for material development, they can include a realistic context for language use in teaching materials and demonstrate it to students. As shown in Table 3.1, some databases are available for Japanese language instruction, but few offer development of material and language education based on practical language data.

There are at least seven databases currently in use. The Computer Assisted System of Teaching and Learning/Japanese (CASTEL/J) (Komatsu et al., 1994; Sakayauchi et al., 1994; Yoshioka et al., 1994; see Chapter 9 of this volume for details) is one of the largest

Database	Notes
1 CASTEL/J	Computer Assisted System for Teaching and Learning/Japanese. <http://www.nier.go.jp/homepage/jouhou/cooperation/index.html> <http://castelj.soken.ac.jp/>
2 JACOP S/F DB	Japanese Conversation Practice Database Indexed by Situation and Function. <http://www.intersc.tsukuba.ac.jp/jacop/>
3 Chu-jokyu Shakai Kagaku-kei Dokkai Kyozai Bank	Reading Materials in Social Sciences
4 Aozora Bunko Kensaku Page	Japanese Literatures Text File Archive and Search (copyright expired) <http://www.aozora.gr.jp/sakuhin.html>
5 Nihon Bungaku Tou Text File	Japanese Literature and Other Text Files <http://kuzan.f-edu.fukui-u.ac.jp/bungaku.htm>
6 Nihon Bungaku Kankei Text File Tou Sakuhin Betsu Gojuuon Jun	Japanese Literature Text File Database Classified with Titles and Authors <http://www.konan-wu.ac.jp/~kikuchi/>
7 Nihon Koten Bungaku Taikei Honbun Database	Japanese Classical Literatures Text Database <http://www.nijl.ac.jp/honmon/index.shtml>

Table 3.1. List of useful databases for Japanese language instruction and research.

databases of Japanese teaching material developed from 1986 on. It includes many text databases, sound resources, pictures, dictionaries, social science books, natural science books, and more. JACOP S/F DB, a Japanese Conversation Practice Database indexed by situation and function, has been developed as a video database using Mpeg files and DVD technology. There is also a *Chu-Jokyu Shakai Kagaku-kei Dokkai Kyozai Bank* (Material Bank of Social Science Readings for Intermediate and Advanced Students), which is distributed to Japanese-language institutions (Himeno et al., 1998). Instructors who teach through Japanese literature can use databases of classical and modern literature. *Aozora Bunko Kensaku Page* (Blue Sky Library Search Page)[1] has works for which copyright has expired or has not been claimed. The *Nihon Koten Bungaku Taikei Hombun Database* (Yasunaga, 1991) is available for classical literature.

Currently, only some databases are open to the public. For instance, the databases of basic Japanese textbooks (Fujita and Yoshioka, 1988, 1990; Oikawa, 1990) and of intermediate textbooks (Yamamoto and Torao, unpublished) are not open because the textbooks are commercial products. However, the Japanese linguistics research bibliography has been open to the public since 23 April 1999.[2]

I have transcribed television drama scenarios and news programs for listening comprehension classes. However, I cannot share these transcriptions or make them available to the public because of copyright restrictions, although I can share statistical data, such as tokens of kanji and vocabulary.

Material Development Tools (MDTs): Calculating *L*

Deciding what to teach (variable L) requires isolation of objectives and of differences between students' knowledge and objectives. Material should fit the individual student as much as possible and should be generated by computer program.

Tool	Name	Function
1	jkwic	Japanese keyword in context
2	unit	Keyword list generator based on dictionary file
3	krf	Kanji reference filter
4	ksf	Kanji statistics filter
5	ngram	Calculator of adjacent characters
6	sp	Item-response matrix calculation program
7	calib	Item and test characteristics calculation program based on the item response theory

Table 3.2. List of material development tools on UNIX platform.

Small programs (Table 3.2) that develop material include "unit (unit extractor)," a word reference processor that divides the text word by word according to a word list, like a dictionary; a kanji reference filter (krf) that divides text by kanji and displays a kanji list with the grade number, from G1 to G6, for elementary school in Japan, or the lesson number in a Japanese textbook; a kanji statistic filter (ksf) that outputs the number of kanji, hiragana, and katakana in a file or files and also outputs the coverage fractions of kanji; and "ngram," which calculates the number of adjacent N-characters in a corpus (N is integer).

However, those who cannot use UNIX or who are not familiar with its commands cannot receive these services. We must find a way to provide the same service for such people. Alternatively, it is possible to use the UNIX system indirectly through e-mail and a browser. An e-mail interface makes output from the system's command very easy to modify and to save as a plain text file. In addition, it should be easy for most e-mail users to handle their own e-mail software anyway. As shown in Table 3.3, various e-mail server systems are available.

Tool	Name	Function
1	Mailgloss	Japanese word glossary auto-generator
2	DejaVu	Kanji statistics calculator and kanji reference list generator
3	SPCalc	Kanji reference filter
4	ksf	SP calculator
5	ikwic	KWIC list display through the Internet

Table 3.3. List of services for e-mail client.

In the rest of this section, I examine four types of MDTs: JKWIC and N-gram on UNIX and Mailgloss and DejaVu on e-mail.

Japanese Keyword in Context (JKWIC)

KWIC is a kind of concordance display of index words. There are many studies and documents concerning KWIC (Kondo, 1991; Ishii, 1992; Ogino and Shiota, 1994; Nakano, 1995). I have made a JKWIC program that enables users to process files which include Japanese two-byte codes and opens to the Internet.

Here is an example using JKWIC with "Japanese Scientific Terms: *Gakujutsu Yougo Shuu*," compiled by the Ministry of Education, Science and Culture, contained in the CASTEL/J CD-ROM. A Chinese student wrote a Japanese composition about his field of study. In it, he used the word "温帯湿潤気候." However, his teacher did not know whether it was Chinese or a technical term. A look into the database revealed that it was a technical term in meteorology as in Figure 3.3. Thus one can check vocabulary in the database and apply the result to improve teaching (Kobayashi, 1999).

```
angel(yamagen)~[324] % jkwic 湿潤  gakujutsu.euc
               : 熱帯湿潤気候
               : 温帯湿潤気候
               : 温帯湿潤気候
               : 陸地湿潤
               : 陸地湿潤気候
                  : 湿潤指数
                  : 湿潤
                  : 湿潤空気
                  : 湿潤冷蔵【球根の】
                  : 湿潤静的エネルギー
                  : 湿潤指数
                  : 湿潤剤
                     ・・・
```

Figure 3.3. Sample use of Japanese Keyword in Context (JKWIC).

N-gram Statistics (*N*-gram) Display Program

A small tool called "*N*-gram" finds collocations in the target text that students want to study. *N*-gram automatically extracts collocations by computation (Kimbrell, 1988; Nagao and Mori, 1994; Ikehara et al., 1995; Maekawa, 1999). In language teaching, *N*-gram statistics show types of expressions and collocations in the target language and apply these techniques to development of materials. Figure 3.4 shows *N*-gram output from the database of television news programs.

```
angel(yamagen)~[127] % ngram  6  news.db | sort | uniq -c | sort -nr | less
      36 ということで
      33 いうことです
      20 たということ
      19 によりますと
      18 となりました
      18 よりますと,
      18 ました. 今日
      13 オウム真理教
      13 ませんでした
      12 こんばんは.
      11 るということ
      11 ました. この
      10 . こんばんは
       9 れましたが,
       9 りましたが,
```

Figure 3.4. Sample output of *N*-gram statistics: six-letter output of television news transcript.

As we can see in the output, we could extract some expressions: - to iu koto desu (ということです), - ni yorimasu to (によりますと), and - to narimashita (となりました), for example, which are helpful for listening to television news programs in the classroom.

Mailgloss

Mailgloss simply sends text by e-mail. First, prepare a text for which you want a glossary. Put one of the following e-mail addresses in the "To:" field, then input text in a "sending message" window of mail software. The original idea of Mailgloss came from Kazumi Hatasa of Purdue University. Henstock and Hatasa (1994) developed AutoGloss/J on the Macintosh platform and coded it in HyperTalk and C. Their intention was to assist procurement of teaching materials, not to provide a language learner's help tool. Generally automatic generation of a glossary by computer may produce some wrong information and different word meanings, because the system does not analyze context. Teaching material should include no mistakes and no misdesign, that is, no confusing information for students learning the language.

I would recommend this system not for students, but for teachers developing material. In 1996, I developed "Wordgloss," a glossary generating program on the UNIX platform, for developing vocabulary lists. In late 1996, with the alias function of the Simple Mail Transport Protocol (SMTP) server system, it became available for those who can handle an e-mail client through the Internet. Now, Mailgloss is available at the sites shown in Table 3.4a. Internally, Mailgloss uses "unit" as a word extractor and the dictionary "Edict," compiled by Jim Breen (Breen, 1996). Table 3.4b shows the procedure of Mailgloss. Figure 3.5a is an example of mail body to send to the system, and Figure 3.5b is a sample list of vocabulary items generated by Mailgloss.

Location	Country	Mail address	Status
Graduate University for Advanced Studies	Japan	<mailgloss@castelj.soken.ac.jp>	primary
University of California, San Diego	USA	<mailgloss@yookoso.ucsd.ac.jp>	secondary
University of Venice	Italy	<mailgloss@iyamato.sni.unive.it>	primary

Table 3.4a. Location and Mailgloss address.

1   Put the address "<mailgloss @castelj.soken.ac.jp>" into the "To:" field of the mailer.
2   Put text prepared as teaching material (as in Figure 3.5a) in the mail body.
3   Put "#BEGIN" (capitals) at the beginning of the text. The text below will be analyzed and looked up in the electronic dictionary. From version 0.98, put "#END" at the end of the data, because many users post mail with their own signature, although I recommended omitting it.
4   In a few minutes you will receive the text that you have just sent and the word list with English translations (Figure 3.5b).

Table 3.4b. Mailgloss procedure.

DejaVu

When using authentic material such as newspaper articles and novels, teachers need to consider their appropriateness for students with regard to the ratio of kana to kanji, sentence length, the ratio of known to unknown vocabulary, expressions, kanji, and so on. Teachers previously had to depend on intuition and experience in selecting text. They could modify material, replacing unknown or difficult words with easy ones known to their students. However, such savvy requires long teaching experience. DejaVu gives teachers kanji information for a text through e-mail. It is available at the sites listed in Table 3.5a. The procedure of DejaVu and the textbook IDs are shown in Table 3.5b and 3.5c. Figure 3.6a is an example of mail body sent to the DejaVu system, and Figure 3.6b is a sample list of kanji items generated by the system.

```
To: mailgloss@intersc.tsukuba.ac.jp
Subject:
--text follows this line--

#BEGIN
これは例です。国立天文台によると、月食は１９９７年９月の皆既月食以来。
来年は１月と７月に皆既月食があるが、日本で見られるのは７月という。
#END
```

Figure 3.5a. Example of mail body to send to Mailgloss system.

```
Date: Sat, 31 Jul 99 03:53:31 JST
Return-Path: mailgloss-sys@intersc.tsukuba.ac.jp
Reply-To: mailgloss-sys@intersc.tsukuba.ac.jp
From: mailgloss-sys@intersc.tsukuba.ac.jp
Subject: mailgloss system message
Apparently-To: yamagen@intersc.tsukuba.ac.jp

=== mailgloss (Version 5.3) ================
これは例です。国立天文台によると、月食は１９９７年９月の皆既月食以来。
来年は１月と７月に皆既月食があるが、日本で見られるのは７月という。

--- glossary ----------------------------
例 [れい] /instance/example/case/precedent/experience/custom/usage/...
国立 [こくりつ] /national/
天文台 [てんもんだい] /astronomical observatory/
によると /according to ../
月食 [げっしょく] /lunar eclipse/
年 [とし] /year/age/
皆既 [かいき] /total eclipse/totality/
以来 [いらい] /since/henceforth/
来年 [らいねん] /next year/
日本 [にほん] /Japan/
```

Figure 3.5b. Sample list of vocabulary items generated by Mailgloss system.

Location	Country	Mail address	Status
Graduate University for Advanced Studies	Japan	\<dejavu @ castelj.soken.ac.jp \>	primary
University of California, San Diego	USA	\<dejavu @yookoso.ucsd.ac.jp\>	secondary
University of Venice	Italy	\<dejavu @iyamato.sni.unive.it\>	primary

Table 3.5a. Location and DejaVu address.

1 Put the address "\<dejavu@castelj.soken.ac.jp\>" into the "To:" field of the mailer.
2 Put text prepared as teaching material (as in Figure 3.6a) in the mail body.
3 Put at least a text ID such as #BKB (i.e., Basic Kanji Book, Vol. 1 and Vol. 2.), a lesson number such as 40, and the #BEGIN and #END commands in the mail body.
4 Write every command with capital letters.
5 A few minutes later, the text will return with the kanji list and the lesson number of the assigned textbook. Or if the kanji is not found in any of the forty-five lessons, a kanji dictionary entry will be shown, as in Figure 3.6b.
6 The textbook IDs appear in Table 3.5c.
7 When only a #HELP or #MAN command appears in the mail body, a manual for DejaVu will be sent.

Table 3.5b. DejaVu procedure.

Text ID	Textbook	Range
BKB	Basic Kanji Book, Vol.1. and Vol.2	1-45
YOOKOSO	Yookoso, Vol. 1	11-17
	Yookoso, Vol. 2	21-27
CMJ	A Course in Modern Japanese	
SHIMBUN (newspaper)	Mainichi Shimbun Newspaper Kanji Frequency	1-2000
GAKUSHUU	Gakushuu Kanji Table	1-6
NNS	The Japanese Language Proficiency Test	1-4

Table 3.5c. Text ID and range parameter.

```
To: dejavu@intersc.tsukuba.ac.jp
Subject:
--text follows this line--

#BKB 40
#BEGIN
さきほど、できたてホヤホヤのデータです。
以下のデータは、言語技能自己評価システムが自動的に
返して来る集計結果です。
#END
```

Figure 3.6a. Example of mail body to send to DejaVu system.

```
Subject: DejaVu System Message (Version 3.2 : 07/19/1999/yamagen)
From: dejavu-sys@intersc.tsukuba.ac.jp
Apparently-To: yamagen@ucsd.edu
Date: Thu, 29 Jul 99 07:24:34 JST

You've looked up Lesson 40 of BKB.
===================== dejavu system =====================
さきほど、できたてホヤホヤのデータです。
以下のデータは、言語技能自己評価システムが自動的に
返して来る集計結果です。

---------------------- kanji list ----------------------
以 [R] イ もっ.て [pn] もち [E] by means of, because, in view of,..
下 4
言 11
語 11
技 [R] ギ わざ [E] skill, art, craft, ability, feat, performance, ..
能 [R] ノウ よ.く [pn] たか の のり よし [E] ability, talent, skill, ..
自 33
己 [R] コ キ おのれ つちのと [pn] し み [E] self, snake, serpent
評 [R] ヒョウ [E] evaluate, criticism, comment
価 35
動 17
的 [R] テキ まと [pn] いくは ゆくは [E] bull's eye, mark, target, ...
返 24
来 9
集 37
計 11
結 25
果 29
```

Figure 3.6b. Sample list of kanji items generated by DejaVu system.

Assessing Students (*I*)

To check students' knowledge and ability (variable *I*), instructors need to conduct a general test. However, testing by paper and pencil takes time. Comparing data for two or three terms and recalculating them on computer is difficult, since the data are not necessarily saved by the instructor in the same format or stored in the same type of storage medium, for example, floppy or hard disc.

To solve these problems, we have been developing application systems that are available on the Web (see Table 3.6). All these applications use the techniques of Common Gateway Interface (CGI) by http protocol on the server computers.[3]

System name	Function
1 Grammar check page	Quiz page generator
2 Grammar tutoring system	Skinner type linear drill generator
3 Diagnostic grammar test	Quiz page generator
4 Kanji reading system	Random item generator for drill and practice
5 Sentence and vocabulary check	Quiz page generator
6 Composition submission page	Revision control and data accumulator of student's compositions

Table 3.6. Web application systems.

We developed two subprograms for analysis of students' response namely, "sp" (a program for calculating item response: scalogram calculation, reproducibility calculation) and "calib" (for calculating item and test characteristics, based on the item-response theory). Further subprograms were "prin-co" (for calculating principal components), factor (for factor analysis), and cluster (for cluster analysis). We modified some programs to calculate web log files directly. Teachers no longer have to input data. The students' responses and behaviour are calculated on the server repeatedly. A detailed feedback report is generated automatically. Via e-mail, teachers receive the report and can grasp the students' traits individually and, on that basis, improve the class and the course itself. Furthermore, data management is easy because students' data is accumulated and appended at the same place and in the same form with a time and date stamp. This is why I recommend client-server computing for language instruction.

Below, I introduce the systems for homework and for self-study, which can be used independently of classroom activities.

Client-Server Grammar Testing System: The Case of DGT

The Diagnostic Grammar Test (DGT) system helps familiarize instructors with students' abilities in Japanese grammar and enables them to detect items of grammar that the students do not know or have not yet learned. This system makes it possible for teachers to give students a test that generates a diagnostic list of their performance, and at the same time, it could serve as a proficiency test at the end of a basic language course or at the beginning of an intermediate course.

The main function of this application is to generate a test web page based on the data bank of test items (itembank.ddf). The web server offers a student differently ordered quiz items each time he or she does a practice run. As soon as they have finished, they receive a diagnostic report from the printer.

In English-language education in Japan, researchers have developed automatic computer generation of a diagnostic profile of English grammar achievement (Takefuta, 1986). Similarly, DGT inputs background data on students' language learning into the database before they gain access to the test page. Students must first answer questions about their own language background before the test begins. The system then calculates the results grouped by the students' profiles.

As shown in Figure 3.7a, DGT has four kinds of databases. All the teacher has to do is register a student's name over the browser for that student to have access to the system.

When students receive their ID and access passwords, they input them at the beginning of the screen page. If they are gaining access for the first time, the system asks them to input their language-learning background data (Figure 3.7b). Students then proceed to the quiz page, where they have five pages to complete. When students have answered all the items, the system at once saves the data and calculates and generates result reports for the student and for the teacher. It sends the report for the student to the network printer and that for the teacher as an e-mail message (Figure 3.7c).

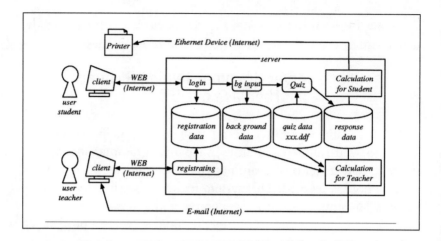

Figure 3.7a. Client-server Diagnostic Grammar Test system.

```
H982078:N1:Lxx_Jxxx_Wxxx
H982078:N2:C315
H982018:BD:1972/09/19
H982018:L1:L340
H982018:L2:L422
H982018:L3:L331
H982018:SY:2
H982018:SH:150
H982018:E1:no
H982018:E2:no
H982018:E3:6
```

Each line has three fields separated by a colon – for personal ID number, for tags, and for values based on the tag in the same line.

N1 name
N2 nationality
BD birthday
L1 first language
L2 second language
L3 third language
SY study years
SH study hours
E1 Can your parent(s) speak Japanese?
E2 Do you use Japanese at home?
E3 How many months are (were) you staying in Japan?

Figure 3.7b. A sample of DGT student language background record database.

```
DGT Diagnostic Table
================================================================
   Category        Achievement Rate                        (%)
                   0   10   20   30   40   50   60   70   80   90  100
                   |----+----+----+----+----+----+----+----+----+----|
   TOTAL SCORE  80 % ooooooooooooooooooooooooooooooooooooooooo
 1 受身         100 % xxxxxxxxxxxxxxxxxxxxxxxxxxxxxxxxxxxxxxxxxxxxxxxxxxx
 2 複文(1)       66 % ooooooooooooooooooooooooooooooooooo
 3 自他          70 % xxxxxxxxxxxxxxxxxxxxxxxxxxxxxxxxxxxxx
 4 複文          57 % oooooooooooooooooooooooooooooo
 5 敬語          63 % xxxxxxxxxxxxxxxxxxxxxxxxxxxxxxxx
 6 敬語         100 % oooooooooooooooooooooooooooooooooooooooooooooooooo
 7 やりもらい    80 % xxxxxxxxxxxxxxxxxxxxxxxxxxxxxxxxxxxxxxxx
 8 疑問詞        90 % oooooooooooooooooooooooooooooooooooooooooooooo
 9 補助動詞      80 % xxxxxxxxxxxxxxxxxxxxxxxxxxxxxxxxxxxxxxxx
10 助詞          78 % oooooooooooooooooooooooooooooooooooooooo
11 比較          70 % xxxxxxxxxxxxxxxxxxxxxxxxxxxxxxxxxxxxx
12 ムード        90 % oooooooooooooooooooooooooooooooooooooooooooooo
13 使役          88 % xxxxxxxxxxxxxxxxxxxxxxxxxxxxxxxxxxxxxxxxxxxxxx
14 可能          90 % oooooooooooooooooooooooooooooooooooooooooooooo
15 活用          90 % xxxxxxxxxxxxxxxxxxxxxxxxxxxxxxxxxxxxxxxxxxxxxx
16 意向          71 % ooooooooooooooooooooooooooooooooooooo
17 アスペクト    87 % xxxxxxxxxxxxxxxxxxxxxxxxxxxxxxxxxxxxxxxxxxxxx
----------------------------------------------------------------
```
1. Passivization; 2. Complex sentences (1); 3. Transitive and intransitive verbs;
4. Complex sentences (2); 5. Complex sentences (3); 6. Honorifics; 7. Giving and
receiving; 8. Interrogatives; 9. Auxiliary verbs; 10. Particles; 11. Comparatives; 12. Mood;
13. Causatives; 14. Potentials; 15. Verb conjugations; 16. Intention; 17. Aspect

Figure 3.7c. Sample of DGT diagnostic table.

The report for the student contains two kinds of information: the diagnostic table shown in Figure 3.7c and a list of incorrectly answered quiz items with the correct answer. Students can use the document for future learning and to correct their weak points.

Client-Server Tutorial System

The Grammar Tutoring System (GTS) is an example of a client-server self-tutorial system. It allows students to acquire knowledge of grammar through small-step quizzes.

As we see on the screen in Figure 3.8, the student answers questions step by step. One question at a time appears on the screen and repeats with a help message until the student can answer it properly. This courseware has a linear stream called "Skinner Type." The structure of the program is simple enough, so that the teacher can modify the quiz database file easily, but the program does not have any clusters or divergent structures.

Figures 3.9a and 3.9b show students' GTS performance tracks during a one-hour lesson. The horizontal axis represents the number of items attempted; the vertical axis, time in seconds. A black dot indicates an incorrect answer, and a white dot, a correct answer.

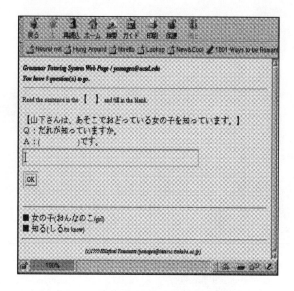

Figure 3.8. Sample web page of Grammar Tutoring System (GTS).

Student A did sixty-four items in about twenty minutes, and student B, sixty-five items in less than forty minutes; both were unable to answer some items in section 3. Using such evidence, instructors can prepare a teaching plan to address students' weak points.

Figure 3.10 shows part of an "error item analysis," calculated from a database on students' performances. "SG200302" is the quiz item ID. It is a section dealing with conditional sentences. "1) *tanomeba* (たのめば)" is the required answer, and 64.3 per cent of the students answered correctly, which is a fairly low percentage. Most students knew the conjugation of the conditional verb but failed to type it properly. The table shows the correct answer and the incorrect answers and the number of students who chose each.

The GTS performance chart and GTS quiz item analysis are also available by browser on demand.

Computers: Curriculum and System Design

Next, we look at two case studies, checking grammar and teaching kanji, focusing on the relationship between computer systems and the curriculum. Coordinating a curriculum with an appropriate computer system will greatly enhance students' learning experiences and facilitate the instructors' teaching.

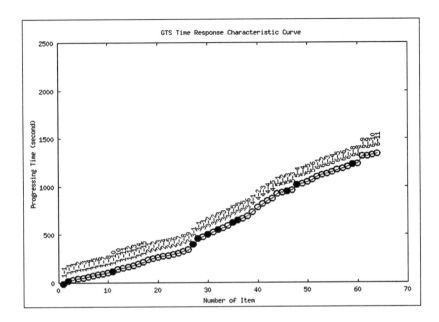

Figure 3.9a. Student's GTS performance in one hour: Student A.
○ correct answer ● incorrect answer

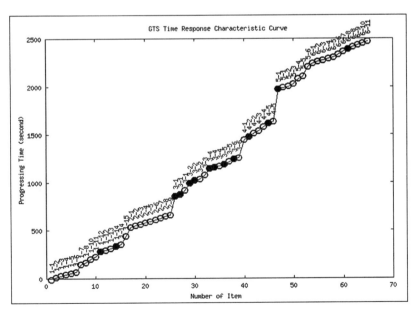

Figure 3.9b. Student's GTS performance in one hour: Student B.
○ correct answer ● incorrect answer

```
SG200302 -----------------------------------------------
1st group verb
アニルさんに頼みます ＋ やってくれます
→アニルさんに（    ）、やってくれます。
 1） たのめば
                              9/ 14 （ 64.3 %)
        たなめば              1
        たにめば              1
        たのまば              1
        たのめば              9
        となめば              1
        なのめば              1
```

Figure 3.10. Sample of GTS error item analysis.

Grammar Check System

The Grammar Check system is one of the web page test genera-tors making the database of test items accessible randomly, like the DGT. In the Japanese language course at the University of Tsukuba, students study new grammar by themselves as homework, and they must learn it before the start of each new lesson. The grammar check system assesses students' knowledge of grammar acquired through self-study and informs the teacher of students' under-standing of the new lesson. Table 3.7 shows the procedure for this system.

Figures 3.11a, 3.11b and 3.11c are samples of the grammar check reports for teachers, which are sent by e-mail every morn-ing at 8:35. Figure 3.11a is a sample of an S-P chart that displays in chart form a student's total score, incorrectly answered items, and discrimination coefficient values (Harnisch, 1983; Sato, 1985; Otsuka, 1986). The teacher can observe who has made many mis-takes and which items students have learned well.

Kanji Teaching

I have been in charge of the kanji class at the University of Tsukuba for two years (1998–2000). In learning kanji today, students need to know the correct kanji reading to input kanji when using a Japanese word processor, and how to use kanji vocabulary correctly. To enhance both aspects, I give students two kinds of homework

1. Before a new lesson, students read grammar notes.
2. Then they go to the web page and check their grammar knowledge.
3. Their learning records are saved in the server system.
4. At once, the system automatically prints out results for each student.
5. At 8:35 a.m. (the class begins at 8:40 a.m.), the system calculates the record and generates a summary report, which describes students' scores, item scores, basic test values, and so on.
6. The summary report goes to class teachers by e-mail.
7. Teachers give students feedback based on the report.
8. Based on the report, instructors cover areas that students do not understand well.

Table 3.7. Basic lesson procedure using the Grammar Check system.

using the web every week. One is the kanji reading system, which is a drill-and-practice system generating quizzes of items randomly from the database file, and the other is the sentence and vocabulary system, which is based on the system for generating test pages mentioned above.

The aim of the kanji class is to enhance memorization of kanji vocabulary through repetitive recall practice. The students must submit web homework by Sunday at 23:59:59. The summary report is then generated and automatically sent to the teacher by e-mail. Table 3.8 demonstrates the procedure for the mid-term and final examinations for the kanji class.

In the third term of my kanji class in 1999, sixteen students were enrolled, and fourteen achieved a grade of sixty per cent or more. The course result was based principally on the average score of the mid-term and the final examinations. Ten students achieved a grade of ninety per cent or more (A), three received eighty per cent or more (B), two were under sixty per cent (D), and one left the course. The text material used was *Basic Kanji Book* (Bonjinsha, 1989), Lessons 23 to 40. A seventy-five-minute class took place once a week for ten weeks, and two to three lessons from the textbook were covered per week in the classroom. A small quiz was conducted every week. Homework consisted of the vocabulary and the reading quizzes for kanji on the web. To complete their homework, students could refer to any source they chose. There were about thirty quiz items on vocabulary per lesson, and about thirty on reading. Consequently, students did about ninety to 120 kanji quiz items per week. I prepared a total of 657 quiz items during the semester. The system calculated students' homework performance

```
Grammar Check Report -- Lesson 01 --
1998/10/17 21:23:45

SP Table ('|'= s, '-'= p, 8 items)
========================================================
              INO
PNO PID       1 2 3 4 5 6 7 8
--------------------------------------------------------
  1 AXxxx     1 1 1 1 1 1 1 1|   8 100.0  0.00
  2 Bxxxxxx   1 1 1 1 1 0|1      7  87.5  0.46
  3 Cxxx      1 1 1 1 1 1 1|0    7  87.5  0.00
  4 Dxxxxx    1 1 1 1 0 1|1_     7  87.5  0.91 *
  5 Exxxxxxx  1 1 1 1 0 1|1      7  87.5  0.91 *
  6 Fxxxx     1 1 1 1 0|1_0      6  75.0  0.30
  7 Gxxxxxxxx 1 1 1 0|1 0 0      5  62.5  0.14
  8 Hxxxxx    1 1 1 1|0_0 0      5  62.5  0.00
  9 Ixxxxxx   1 1 1 0|1 0 0      5  62.5  0.14
 10 Jxxxxxx   1_0_1_0|1 1 0      4  50.0  0.46
 11 Kxxxxx    0 1 0 0|1 1 1 0    4  50.0  1.08 **
 12 Lxxxxx    0|0 0 0 0 1 0 0    1  12.5  1.23 **
 13 Mxxxxx    0|0 0 1 0 0 0 0    1  12.5  0.00
```

Figure 3.11a. Sample of Grammar Check report for instructors: S-P chart.

```
Item Data Description
========================================================
INO IID        SUM   NUM   MEAN   COEF
--------------------------------------------------------
  1 GC0108      17    20   0.85   0.81 *
  2 GC0105      15    20   0.75   0.22
  3 GC0103      13    20   0.65   0.30
  4 GC0101      12    20   0.60   0.17
  5 GC0107      11    20   0.55   0.38
  6 GC0106      11    20   0.55   0.16
  7 GC0102      10    20   0.50   0.15
  8 GC0104       5    20   0.25   0.36
```

Figure 3.11b. Sample of Grammar Check report for instructors: item result.

```
Test Values(%)
========================================================
              Person              Item
--------------------------------------------------------
number        12                  31
average       22.33( 72.04)        8.65( 72.04)
minimum        4   ( 12.90)        3  ( 25.00)
maximum       29   ( 93.55)       11  ( 91.67)
std.dev.       6.64                2.40


Reproducibility
========================================================
Rep:coefficient of reproducibility           0.84
mmRep:minimum marginal reproducibility        0.72
Guttman:coefficient of scalability            0.42
```

Figure 3.11c. Sample Grammar Check report for instructors: test value calculation.

1. Students submit as homework two web practices before midnight every Sunday.
2. The system sends a summary report to the teacher by e-mail.
3. The teacher analyzes quiz items.
4. The teacher excludes quiz items that are not appropriate according to data analysis.
5. The teacher generates the test by selecting low-scored items.
6. The teacher conducts the mid-term or the final examination.
7. The system prints out feedback report sheets for students and a summary report sheet for the teacher.
8. When their score is under ninety per cent, students must take the same test again a few days later.

Table 3.8. The procedure of mid-term and final examinations for kanji class.

at 6:00 a.m. every morning and sent the results to the teacher. Mistakes and errors were dealt with in the classroom.

Items that received incorrect answers in homework were selected from the item database. Items judged defective by analysis of home-work performance log files were eliminated from the list. Two tests took place as mid-term and final examinations. Students whose score was under ninety per cent took the same test again until they achieved ninety per cent. As a result, every student achieved a higher than ninety per cent performance for kanji and vocabulary.

Discussion

Client-server language teaching has a number of merits, but also some problems that should be taken into account.

In terms of budgeting for human resources, we need at least five people steeped in language education: a computer maintenance and development technician, a database developer, a manual writer, an orientation presenter for students, and a workshop coordinator for instructors. If the budget is insufficient, the language teacher must act as a database developer, a manual writer, an orientation presenter, a workshop coordinator—and, if possible, a computer technician!

One might imagine that technology would improve a course, but unfortunately that is not necessarily the case. Once a student takes a seat in front of the computer, many unexpected things occur. The computer can even hinder language learning. Accordingly, we need to consider our priorities for successful installation of computer-assisted language learning (CALL). The maximum effect of learn-ing (*Emax*) is a function (*f*) of five factors: administration (*A*), database (*D*), financial support (*F*), technology (*T*), and students' characteristics (*S*). Thus

$$Emax = f(A, D, F, T, S).$$

Problems or inadequacies in any factor will create difficulties, as the following examples show. For instance, if a teacher does not have the budget (*F*) to buy computers for the students, he or she must limit use of computer technology to managing marks and preparing for classes, as in materials development. In another example, when there is no database or no corpus of material (*D*) in the target language, the teacher needs to develop the database, which is the most precious dimension of the computer resources. When there are no data, use of a computer makes no sense, even if it has a very fancy program. Further, when the aptitude and readiness of students (*S*) are low, the teacher addresses deficiencies by setting appropriate goals as part of program administration (*A*). In that case, even if there is a person who knows computer technology (*T*), technology itself is insufficient.

Conclusion

In conclusion, a client-server CMI system can mediate effectively between students and teachers in language-learning courses. A system for language instruction should not be ad hoc, as we see in some commercial software, but must be an exact fit for and be based on the curriculum of the actual language course. The instructor must understand the system's use and agree with colleagues on implementation, matching curriculum with system use. As described, many software tools are available for consideration in this process.

For the future, I would emphasize four points. Clarify the elements of education that are indispensable. Switch over to technology-based education only over a reasonably long period of transition. Develop a mechanism that includes an evaluation system. Carry out research in the technology of language education until its results are practical and useful.

Acknowledgments

I wish to thank my colleagues at the University of Tsukuba for their assistance: Stefan Kaiser, who worked on the JACOP-DB project, English check, and provided many useful comments, Chieko Kano, who worked on kanji education and database, Noriko Kobayashi, for development of the testing program; Yoshimi Nishimura, who worked on the Japanese tutorial system; and Takao Kinugawa, who worked on composition editing system and client services management. Thanks also to Yashy Tohsaku, University of California at San Diego, for giving me the chance to develop my first client-server system of language instruction.

Notes

1. <http://www.voyager.co.jp/aozora/main.html>
2. <http://www2.kokken.go.jp/kokugokw /bunkenkw.html>
3. Generally most of them are written in Perl. The author also uses Perl as a programming language except for internal student data calculations that are written in C.

References

Breen, J.W. 1996. The Document File of EDICT Freeware Japanese/ English Dictionary File.

Brudner, J.J. 1998. "Computer-Managed Instruction." *Science*, 162: 970–6.

Fujita, M., and R. Yoshioka. 1988. *Shokyu nihongo kyokasho no goi* (Vocabulary in Japanese Elementary Textbooks). In *Paso-com ni yoru gaikokujin no tame no nihongo kyouiku shien system no kaihatsu* (Development of Computer Assisted Instruction System for Japanese as a Second Language). Research Report. Grant-in-Aid Program for Developmental Scientific Research, Ministry of Education, Science, Sports and Culture. 26–37.

Fujita, M., and R. Yoshioka. 1990. *Nihongo kyokasho goi list no bunseki* (Analysis of Vocabulary in Japanese Textbooks). In *Paso-com ni yoru gaikokujin no tame no nihongo kyouiku shien system no kaihatsu* (Development of Computer Assisted Instruction System for Japanese as a Second Language). Research Report. Grant-in-

Aid Program for Developmental Scientific Research, Ministry of Education, Science, Sports and Culture, 103–12.

Glaser, R. 1967. "Adapting the Elementary School Curriculum to Individual Performance." In *Proceedings for the 1967 Invitational Conference on Testing Problems*, 3–36. Princeton, NJ: Educational Testing Service.

Harnisch, D.L. 1983. "Item Response Patterns: Applications for Educational Practice," *Journal of Educational Measurement* 20, no. 2: 191–206.

Henstock, P., and K. Hatasa. 1994. *Autogloss/J: Automatic Glossary Generation for Japanese Text* (software program). Purdue: Purdue University.

Himeno, M., et al. 1998. *Chou joo kyuu syakai kagaku kei dokkai kyoozai bank* (Material Bank for Intermediate and Advanced Level Students of Social Science). Tokyo: The Japanese Language Center for International Students, Tokyo University of Foreign Studies.

Ikehara, S., S. Shirai, and T. Kawaoka. 1995. "Automatic Extraction of Uninterrupted and Interrupted Collocations from Very Large Japanese Corpora Using E-gram Statistics." *Journal of Information Processing* 36, no. 11: 2584–96.

Ishii, M. 1992. *Program o kakazu ni dekiru gengo shori - Editor de hindo hyo, Kwic, shooroku-bun o tsukuru* (Language processing without Programming—Making Word Frequency Table, kwic Abstract Using Text Editing Software). *Nihongo Gaku* 11, no. 9: 114–24.

Kimbrell, R.E. 1988. "Searching for Text? Send an *N*-gram!" (includes related articles on implementing *N*-gram systems and *N*-gram vectors) (technical). *Byte* 13, no. 5: 297–306.

Kobayashi, N. 1999. Personal communication.

Komatsu, Y., M. Sakayauchi, and R. Yoshioka. 1994. "CASTEL/J: Development of a Computer Assisted System for Teaching and Learning Japanese (3) Multimedia Database." *The Fourth Conference of the Society for Japan Educational Technology* 1, 331–32.

Kondo, Y. 1991. *Koten bumpou no tachiba kara kangaeta 'kensaku' to 'text'* (Search and Text for Japanese Classic Grammar). *Nihongo Gaku* 10, no. 11: 104–14.

Lindvall, C.M., and J.O. Bolvin. 1967. "Programmed Instruction in the Schools: An Application of Programming Principles in 'Individually Prescribed Instruction.'" In P. Lange, ed., *Programmed Instruction*, 1st ed., 217–54. Chicago: University of Chicago Press.

Maekawa, M. 1999. *Bunsho o tsukuru: moji to moji no kankei koji sokan* (Generation of Sentences and Phrases: High Relations between Characters). In *1000 man-nin no computer kagaku* (Computer Science for Ten Million People) *3—Bungaku hen* (Literatures), 74–5. Tokyo: Iwanami Shoten.

Nagao, M., and S. Mori. 1994. "A New Method of *N*-gram Statistics for Large Numbers of *N* and Automatic Extraction of Words and Phrases from Large Text Data of Japanese." In *Proceedings of the Fifteenth International Conference on Computational Linguistics*, 611–15.

Nakano, H. 1995. *Pasokon riyoo no genjoo to kadai 'goi'* (The Present Situation and Issues Using Computers: 'Vocabulary'). *Nihongo Gaku* 14, no. 8 (July special issue): 40–52.

Nakano, H. 1996. *Pasokon ni yoru nihongo kenkyuu hou nyuumon* (An Introduction to Japanese Research Method Using a Personal Computer). Tokyo: Kazama Shoin.

Ogino, T. 1981. *Computer ga egaku gengo chizu* (Language Map by Computer). *Gengo* 10, no. 10: 56–61.

Ogino, T., and T. Shiota. 1994. *Asahi shimbun database o riyooshita gengo kenkyou* (Language Analysis Using Asahi Newspaper Database). *Nihongo Gaku* 13, no. 5: 28–39.

Oikawa, A. 1990. *Kenkyu keika houkoku* (Interim Research Report). In *Paso-con ni yoru gaikokujin no tame no nihongo kyouiku shien shisutemu no kaihatsu* (Development of Computer Assisted Instruction System for Japanese as a Second Language). Research Report. Grant-in-Aid Program for Developmental Scientific Research, Ministry of Education, Science, Sports and Culture, 1–22.

Otsuka, Y. 1986. *Test komoku no kozo o saguru: S-P hyo, shakudo kaiseki* (Analysis of Test Item Structure: SP-chart, Analysis of Scalability). In H. Kaiho, ed., *Shinri kyoiku data no kaiseki hou 10 kou* (Analysis Methods of Psychological and Educational Data. 10 Courses), 1st ed. 54–76. Tokyo: Fukumura Shuppan.

Sakayauchi, M., R. Yoshioka, and Y. Komatsu. 1994. "CASTEL/J: Development of a Computer Assisted System for Teaching and Learning Japanese (1)." In *The Fourth Conference of the Society for Japan Educational Technology*. 327–8.

Sato, T. 1985. *S-P hyo nyumon* (An Introduction to the S-P Chart). Tokyo: Meiji Tosho.

Takefuta, Y. 1986. *Eigo kyooshi no pasokon* (Personal Computers for English Teachers). Tokyo: Educa Shuppan.

Yamamoto, H. and Y. Torao, 2000. Japanese Textbook Database, unpublished.

Yasunaga, H. 1991. *Nihon koten bungaku hombun database* (Text Database of Japanese Classic Literature). *Nihongo Gaku* 10, no. 8: 67–77.

Yoshioka, R., Y. Komatsu, and M. Sakayauchi. 1994. "CASTEL/J: Development of a Computer Assisted System for Teaching and Learning Japanese (2)—Dictionary and Text Database." *Conference of the Society for Japan Educational Technology 1*, 329-30.

Appendix

List of computer programs and database projects

Abbreviations:

UNIX: UNIX applications
SMTP: SMTP protocol applications
HTTP: HTTP protocol applications
PROJ: Project web sites and information

1. jkwic (UNIX)
   Japanese keyword in context display program.
   http://aci-japan.soken.ac.jp/users/yamagen/jk/
2. unit (UNIX)
   Keyword list generator based on Japanese-English dictionary.
   http://aci-japan.soken.ac.jp/users/yamagen/unit/
3. krf (UNIX)
   Kanji reference filter.
   http://aci-japan.soken.ac.jp/users/yamagen/krf/
4. ksf (UNIX)
   Kanji statistics filter.
   http://aci-japan.soken.ac.jp/users/yamagen/ksf/
5. ngram (UNIX)
   Calculator of adjacent characters.
   http://aci-japan.soken.ac.jp/users/yamagen/ngram/

6. sp (UNIX)
   Item-response matrix calculation program.
   http://aci-japan.soken.ac.jp/users/yamagen/sp/
7. calib (UNIX)
   Item and test characteristics calculation program
   based on the item response theory
   http://aci-japan.soken.ac.jp/users/yamagen/calib/
8. Mailgloss (SMTP)
   Japanese word glossary auto-generator.
   mailto:mailgloss@castelj.soken.ac.jp
   http://aci-japan.soken.ac.jp/users/yamagen/mg/
9. DejaVu (SMTP)
   Kanji statistics calculator and kanji reference list generator.
   mailto:dejavu@castelj.soken.ac.jp
   http://aci-japan.soken.ac.jp/users/yamagen/dv/
10. SPCalc (SMTP)
    SP table calculator.
    mailto:spcalc@castelj.soken.ac.jp
    http://aci-japan.soken.ac.jp/users/yamagen/sp/
11. ksf (SMTP)
    Kanji reference filter.
    mailto:ksf@castelj.soken.ac.jp
    http://aci-japan.soken.ac.jp/users/yamagen/ksf/
12. ikwic (SMTP)
    KWIC list display through Internet
    mailto:ikwic@castelj.soken.ac.jp
    http://aci-japan.soken.ac.jp/users/yamagen/ik/
13. Grammar check page (HTTP)
    Grammar quiz page generator.
    http://aci-japan.soken.ac.jp/users/yamagen/gc/
14. Grammar tutoring system (HTTP)
    Skinner type linear drill generator.
    http://aci-japan.soken.ac.jp/users/yamagen/gts/
15. Diagnostic grammar test (HTTP)
    Quiz page generator.
    http://aci-japan.soken.ac.jp/users/yamagen/dgt/
16. Kanji reading system (HTTP)
    Random item generator for drill and practice.
    http://aci-japan.soken.ac.jp/users/yamagen/kr/

17. Sentence and vocabulary check system (HTTP)
Quiz page generator.
http://aci-japan.soken.ac.jp/users/yamagen/sv/
18. Composition submission system (HTTP)
Revision control and data accumulator of student's compositions.
http://aci-japan.soken.ac.jp/users/yamagen/css/
19. JACOP Project (PROJ)
Japanese Conversation Practice Database Streaming Video Clip
Project. The project began in 1994 at University of Tsukuba
to develop computer video files for Japanese language teaching.
Streaming video resources are available via Internet.
http://aci-japan.soken.ac.jp/groups/jacop/
20. Sakyo Komatsu Corpus Project (PROJ)
The project is for the database development of all works of Sakyo
Komatsu, a Japanese science-fiction writer. On the web-site, users
can search Japanese expression with Japanese KWIC search engine.
The same set of database is also included in CASTEL/J
Millennium CD-ROM with Japanese KWIC program.
http://castelj.soken.ac.jp/groups/komatsu/
21. Thumbnail Japanese Picture Search Engine Project (PROJ)
This web site is for the picture database, which users can search for
pictures they want to use in their classroom. The search result
shows thumbnail pictures with Japanese sentences. CASTEL/J
Millennium CD-ROM also contains the same series of pictures.
http://castelj.soken.ac.jp/groups/thumb_nail/
22. Academic Japanese and Applications Project (PROJ)
Teaching Resource Center for Academic Japanese based on
Bare Bone Database system.
http://aci-japan.soken.ac.jp/groups/aj/
23. BB-DB Bare Bone Database Project (PROJ)
BB-DB includes the basic solutions of the database I have
been developing.
http://aci-japan.soken.ac.jp/groups/bbdb/

For inquiries, contact the author at:
<http://aci-japan.soken.ac.jp/users/yamagen/>
<http://cupid.ucsd.edu/~yamagen/>

Analyzing Japanese Textbooks Using the Vocabulary and Kanji Level Checker

Yoshiko Kawamura

In this chapter, I discuss how to use information technology to analyze Japanese language textbooks. First, I report in some detail on the Vocabulary Level Checker (VLC) and the Kanji Level Checker (KLC) programs. Both checkers were developed to estimate the level of difficulty of Japanese reading material. The VLC automatically divides a text into words and shows the level of each word according to the Japanese Language Proficiency Test (JLPT). Similarly, the KLC shows the level of each kanji according to the JLPT. Second, I report the results of a pilot project to test the usefulness of both checkers. This project analyzed eight Japanese textbooks (see Appendix for titles) using the two checkers to correlate the difficulty of vocabulary and kanji with the supposed level of reading materials. Finally, I discuss the results of the analysis.

Background

Computer technology has affected all areas of education, including the study of foreign languages. In Japan, research and teaching in Japanese as a foreign or second language (JFL/JSL) has made major advances since the 1980s using these technologies.[1] The effort has included collection of large electronic databases as well as development of computerized teaching systems. Japan's National Institute for Educational Research developed one of the earliest large-scale databases for Japanese reading materials, CASTEL/J.[2] Materials from CASTEL/J were then used to develop the *Shinsho Library*.[3] The Foreign Student Education Center of Tokyo University of Foreign Studies developed another major resource bank containing reading material from the social sciences.[4]

These carefully constructed resource banks or databases offer valuable resources for teachers and researchers alike. However, their construction requires an enormous quantity of material and a great deal of labour. Although the need for them has been recognized, problems related to development and funding still remain.

Circumstances have begun to change recently. Rapid diffusion of the Internet has made acquisition of large amounts of electronic data possible. With access to good learning support via the Internet, students can choose the kind of reading material they need. Independent researchers recognize the Internet's potential and have developed tools to support independent study. Tera, Kitamura, and Ochimizu (1996) developed "the reading comprehension support system DL (dictionary linking system)," which automatically shows the reading of each kanji and the meaning of each word in a text. Kitamura also developed FG (kanji *furigana* tool), which shows the reading of each kanji combination (Kawamura and Kitamura, 1998). The DL and the FG are available to the public free of charge over the Internet.[5] Taking this project one step further, Kawamura, Kitamura, and Hobara (2000) used a large digital Japanese-English dictionary in the development of the Dictionary Tool. This is also available via the Internet.[6] The Dictionary Tool incorporates a system for reporting a learner's progress to help both learners and instructors track vocabulary development. Another useful tool, the kanji learning system JUPITER developed by Ochi et al. (1997), picks out important kanji idioms in a text and automatically generates a kanji quiz.[7] In short, an Internet-based language learning environment is being created.

I integrated the features of several of these tools and developed the Level Checker, which automatically estimates the level of difficulty of Japanese reading material. It analyzes each element in a given text and indexes its difficulty using a level checker for vocabulary, kanji, and grammatical structure. Planned future versions will synthesize the results of all three dimensions and give a rating for level of difficulty.

The Vocabulary Level Checker (VLC) has a morphological parser called "ChaSen" that divides a text into words. It compares all the words in the text with the words in lists taken from the four levels in the Japanese Language Proficiency Test (JLPT)[8] and shows the level of each word. Similarly, the Kanji Level Checker (KLC) shows the level of each kanji according to the JLPT. They index every word and kanji that appear in a set of Japanese textbooks for various levels, elementary, intermediate, and advanced, according to the JLPT level of difficulty, and then analyze the percentage of words and kanji in each level.

The following section explains the structures of the VLC and the KLC, demonstrates how to use the results of the analysis of the two checkers, and reports the results of the analysis of eight Japanese textbooks using the VLC and the KLC.

Structure

The Vocabulary Level Checker

The VLC automatically indexes the level of difficulty of all the words in a Japanese text by comparing them with the words in the lists taken from the four levels of the JLPT (Kawamura, 1998). Nation (1990) developed a software program for English in which a computer automatically indexes the frequency level of all the words in a text.[9] However, such a computer program has not been developed for Japanese until now. The Japanese language is normally written or printed without spaces between words, so it is difficult for a computer to judge the physical boundaries of each word. The VLC extracts all the words in a text by using the morphological parser *ChaSen*[10] and then indexes the level of difficulty of every word.

Figure 4.1 shows the input screen of the VLC. The user types text into the text box or can "copy and paste" text from the Internet. He or she then clicks the "Enter" button, and the program analyzes the text in five ways:

- A morphological analysis divides the text into words.
- The program compares words in the text against words in the four levels of the JLPT.
- It indicates the level of each word in the text.
- It prepares a table of words divided into levels.
- It calculates the number/percentage of words in each level.

Figure 4.2 shows the output screen of the VLC. The text analyzed here is the first part of Lesson 1 in an intermediate Japanese

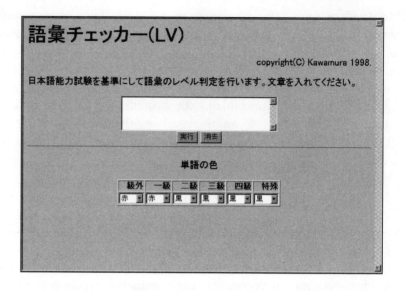

Figure 4.1. Input screen of the VLC.

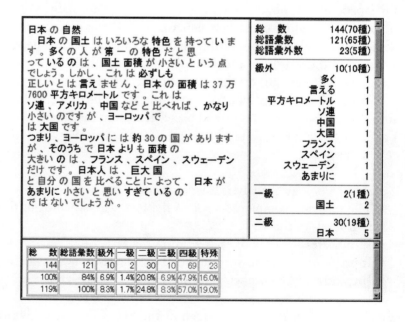

Figure 4.2. Output screen of the VLC.

textbook.[11] The resulting page contains three components. The upper left of the screen is the marked text analyzed by the VLC with all words at the intermediate level (level 2) and higher highlighted. The user can, however, change these settings with the colour buttons. In the upper right frame, all the words in the text appear in a long list divided into the four levels of the JLPT. Learners and teachers can use these lists as vocabulary lists. The table at the bottom shows the number of words and the percentage in each class. With this table, the user can see the percentage of unknown words for a particular group of learners at a glance. Teachers can use the table to select appropriate material for students. It can also provide data about how many words at each level appear in the text. In short, the VLC is useful not only for learners and teachers but also for researchers who want to investigate the readability of a text.

The Kanji Level Checker

The KLC is a program that analyzes the JLPT level of difficulty of all kanji in a text.[12] It performs the following operations automatically:

- The program compares each kanji in the text against kanji in the four levels of the JLPT.
- It indicates the level of each kanji in the text.
- It prepares a table of words divided into levels.
- It calculates the number/percentage of kanji in each level.

Figure 4.3 represents KLC's output screen. The colour-coded text appears in the upper-left area of the output screen. The KLC highlights all the kanji at the intermediate level (level 2) and higher. The classification table of the kanji, divided into JLPT levels, appears in the upper-right area. The table at the bottom shows the number of kanji and the percentage for each level.

Using the Output Screens

With the VLC, students can see at a glance how many unknown words the reading material contains. The VLC generates a list (which appears on the right-hand side of the screen) of all unknown words or words of each level, and it also colour-codes the text itself; words

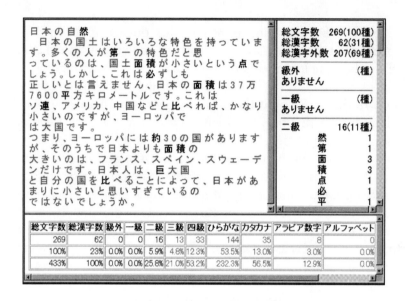

in level 1 are red, level 2 are green, and so on. A text that contains many words beyond the student's proficiency level not only looks colourful on the screen, but also reminds the instructor of the difficulty the student is experiencing.

Choosing white for colour-coding allows the teacher to "white out," or hide, all words at any level and higher. In Figure 4.4, all words at level 2 (intermediate) and higher are hidden. Students can either be asked to fill in these spaces or be given several words to choose from to fill in the blanks. They can also check the vocabulary themselves before and after studying a given text.

Highlighting unknown words allows learners to guess the meaning from the context and to develop other strategies for guessing meanings. However, when there are too many unknown words, guessing all of them may be impossible, especially for students from countries that do not use kanji. Figure 4.4, in which the VLC hides words at the intermediate level and higher, shows the difficulty of this sample text for students.

Figure 4.5 is an example of the KLC output screen that analyzed the same material as Figure 4.4. It hides kanji at the intermediate level and higher. By comparing Figures 4.4 and 4.5, we see that the text in Figure 4.5 is considerably more readable. Even with some

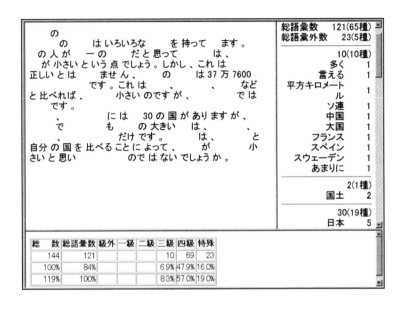

Figure 4.4. The VLC output screen, with all words at level 2 and higher hidden.

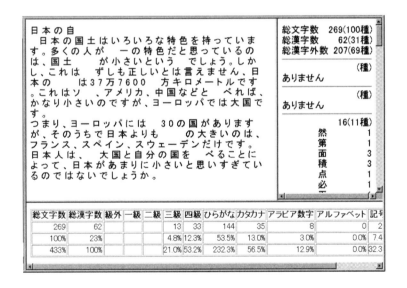

Figure 4.5. The KLC output screen, with all kanji at level 2 and higher hidden.

kanji removed, it is not difficult to read and understand the outline of this text. What does this difference tell us?

The analyzed text contains forty-two words from level 2 and higher, or 34.8 per cent of all the words in the text. When students do not know or cannot guess the meaning of these words, they cannot read the text. However, seeing the number of unknown kanji creates a different situation. The text contains sixteen kanji from level 2 and higher, only 5.9 per cent of all the letters in the text. Even this proportion of unknown kanji should not inhibit comprehension. When the lists of the JLPT serve as a standard for choosing reading material, the level of readability will differ greatly, depending on whether the list of vocabulary or that of kanji is used. The output screens of the VLC and the KLC clearly show this difference.

An Analysis of Japanese Textbooks

Using the VLC

To determine the difficulty of reading materials, I now report the results of an analysis of Japanese textbooks using the VLC (Kawamura, 1999). I analyzed eight Japanese textbooks to determine the relationship between the supposed difficulty level of the texts and the level of vocabulary according to the JLPT. I selected textbooks published in Japan and commonly used in Japanese language schools and universities: four elementary, three intermediate, and one advanced. I divided each textbook into three parts, and then scanned and analyzed several lessons from each part with the VLC.

The number of letters in the material from each textbook level used in this investigation are as follows: elementary, 7,311; intermediate, 14,067; and advanced, 16,749. Morphological analysis showed the total numbers of words as: elementary, 3,068; intermediate, 6,547; and advanced, 7,776.

If there is a correlation between the difficulty of a text and that of the number of words in it, we should be able to make two hypotheses. *Hypothesis 1*: As the difficulty of reading material increases, the percentage of easy words should decrease. *Hypothesis 2*: As the difficulty of material increases, so should the percentage of difficult words.

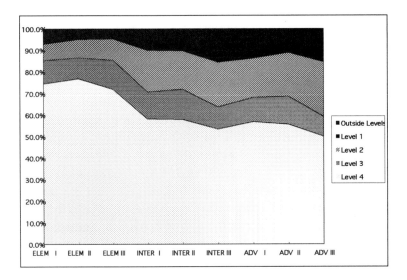

Figure 4.6. VLC analysis of words in Japanese textbooks.

Figure 4.6 presents the result of the analysis. The two highest levels of vocabulary tend to increase along with the difficulty of the textbooks. Level 3 remains constant at about ten per cent across all reading levels. The lowest level (level 4) decreases with the difficulty of the textbooks. Words outside the levels tend to increase slightly with the difficulty of the textbooks.

The Pearson correlation coefficient was $r = 0.74$ ($N = 34$) for words from level 4, with a negative correlation recognized. Hypothesis 1 was verified. The correlation coefficient for words at level 2 was $r = 0.82$, with a high positive correlation. Furthermore, words at level 1 received a higher positive correlation ($r = 0.86$). Hypothesis 2 was also proven for the two highest levels.

In contrast, the correlation coefficient of words outside the levels was low, with $r = 0.21$. Even in the elementary textbooks, about five per cent of the words are outside the levels, mostly proper nouns, which rarely appear on the JLPT word list. However, a proper noun is not difficult for learners if they know how to pronounce it. Proper nouns may appear frequently, even in an elementary textbook, for example, in a chapter on self-introduction. Clearly we need to consider the number of proper nouns in a given text before deciding on the level of difficulty of words.

Figure 4.6 also reveals a remarkable increase in unknown words from the elementary to the intermediate level. In elementary textbooks, unknown words (level 2 and higher) number about fifteen per cent. The intermediate textbooks contain thirty per cent. The percentage of unknown words increases only slightly, however, between intermediate and advanced levels. Clearly, the intermediate level will be quite difficult for beginning students.

In the advanced textbook, the proportion of unknown words for advanced-level students (level 1 and higher) is about fifteen per cent. This is lower than the proportion of unknown words in the intermediate textbook. However, fifteen per cent is still high, and each reading in the advanced textbook is long. If students do not have strategies for guessing meanings, they will not be able to complete a reading assignment.

The VLC analysis shows not only the relation between the supposed level of difficulty of texts and the level of vocabulary, but also the need to consider the vocabulary level from the viewpoint of student knowledge when choosing reading material.

Using the KLC

I analyzed eight Japanese textbooks in order to determine the relation between the estimated level of difficulty of texts and the level of kanji according to the JLPT. Three correlations may hold. *Hypothesis 1*: As the difficulty of the reading material increases, the percentage of kanji increases. *Hypothesis 2*: As the difficulty of the reading material increases, the proportion of easy kanji decreases. *Hypothesis 3*: As the difficulty of the reading material increases, so does the proportion of difficult kanji.

Figure 4.7 and 4.8 present the results of the KLC's analysis (Kawamura, 1999). Figure 4.7 shows that the percentage of kanji in a text tends to increase along with the difficulty of the textbooks. The Pearson correlation coefficient was $r = 0.73$ ($N = 34$) for the percentage of all the kanji in each text, with a positive correlation. Hypothesis 1 was verified.

We can infer five statements from Figure 4.8. The lowest level kanji (level 4) decrease with the difficulty of the textbooks. Level 3 is fixed at about thirty per cent. Level 2 tends to increase with the difficulty of the textbooks. The highest level (level 1) tends to increase

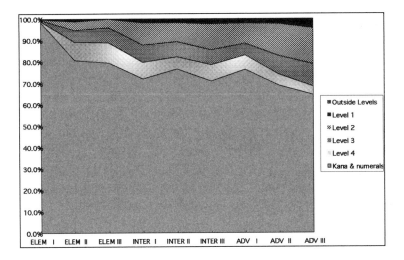

Figure 4.7. KLC analysis of words in Japanese textbooks.

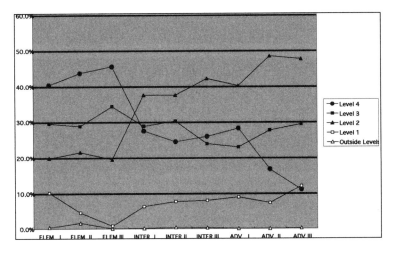

Figure 4.8. Levels of kanji (%) in Japanese textbooks.

slightly along with the difficulty of the textbooks; the highest level kanji constitute ten per cent of all kanji, even at the primary level. Textbooks in all levels contain very few kanji outside the levels.

The Pearson correlation coefficient was $r = 0.43$ for kanji of level 4, with a weak negative correlation. However, we cannot declare hypothesis 2 verified. The correlation coefficient for kanji of level 2 was $r = 0.81$, with a high plus correlation. Hypothesis 3 is then proven for level 2. As for kanji of level 1, the correlation coefficient for kanji of level 2 was $r = 0.32$, with only a weak correlation. This is because there are several level 1 kanji even in the first part of some elementary textbooks. Each kanji there is accompanied with the reading (*furigana*), which allows writers to use many kanji without being selective. It may be necessary to conduct a more specified investigation of textbooks in two categories: those with *furigana* readings and those without.

Kanji outside the levels rarely appear in any of the textbook levels. The JLPT levels cover the most commonly used kanji recognized officially by the Ministry of Education (*jouyou* kanji). This result is different from that of the analysis with the VLC; about fifteen per cent of the words in an advanced text are unknown even for advanced students, and about ten per cent are outside the levels. In the analysis of Japanese reading material, the KLC and the VLC will produce different level counts.

If students learn all the kanji up to level 1, that is, all the *jouyou*-kanji, and know their readings and meanings, they may think that they can read all Japanese reading material. However, this is not necessarily true. As each kanji generally has more than two readings, and sometimes several meanings, one can determine its reading and meaning only by looking at the combination of kanji and the context of each. Comparison of our two results reveals that even if students "know" every kanji in a reading passage, they may not know the meaning of each combination. They must learn how to guess and grasp the meaning of unknown words using their knowledge of similar words and of component kanji.

Conclusion

Analysis of eight Japanese textbooks using the VLC revealed a general correlation between the supposed level of difficulty of a textbook and its vocabulary. The elementary textbooks generally contain easy, familiar words and the intermediate and advanced levels contain many unknown words for students at these two levels. However, the analysis also showed a significant difference in the amount of difficult vocabulary between elementary and intermediate textbooks. This underlines the need to consider the students' knowledge of vocabulary when choosing reading material.

Analysis with the KLC revealed a similar correlation between the supposed difficulty of a textbook and the difficulty of kanji. The percentage of kanji in a text and the total number of higher-level kanji tend to increase with the difficulty of the textbook. However, comparing these two analyses suggests the need to carefully consider the difficulty of both kanji and vocabulary when choosing Japanese reading material. It also clarifies the need to teach students how to guess the meaning of unknown words.

The final goal of the VLC and the KLC is to create an automatic level-estimating system for reading material. We intended the pilot project discussed above to investigate the relation between the difficulty of reading material and that of vocabulary and kanji. We analyzed only random parts of eight textbooks. Extensive investigation should be done with more Japanese textbooks. Furthermore, as I mentioned previously, the VLC and the KLC use the JLPT lists as a standard for reading levels. The results might be different for other standards. Investigating many kinds of reading materials using the JLPT, and other standards as well, should help us to find a more accurate standard. The Level Checker[13] will incorporate the results of further investigation.

Notes

1. Developments in technology have greatly influenced JFL/JSL theories of learning and teaching. Language education in Japan has begun to incorporate more of the principles of the "learner-centred" approach (Tanaka, 1988), which has also influenced the development of resource bank and resource centres.
2. CASTEL/J database consists of reading materials, scripts of movies, and dictionaries. It is available on CD-ROM (Asakimori, 1994). See Chapter 9 of this volume for details.
3. *Shinsho Library* was developed with reading materials from CASTEL/J. Its dictionary function offers English translation, Japanese synonyms and antonyms, and word usage (Kijima and Shimizu, 1998; Suzuki, 1998). See Chapter 7 of this volume for details.
4. Ninety-two intermediate and advanced-level materials were collected for a text bank. Every text is accompanied with a word list, an idiom list, sentence patterns, commentaries, and exercises (Foreign Student Education Center, 1998).

5. A newer version of the DL, the DLII, incorporates a system for reporting a learner's progress to help both learners and instructors track vocabulary development. The DLII is also available at http://language.tiu.ac.jp/~kitamura (Kitamura et al., 1999a, 1999b).

6. The Dictionary Tool and the Level Checker are part of the Japanese Language Reading Tutorial System, "Reading Tutor," which is available over the Internet at <http://language.tiu.ac.jp> (Kawamura et al., 1999).

7. The *furigana* reading function of this learning system, known as Kanji Ruby, is distributed as freeware on the Internet <http://n51.is.tokushima-u.ac.jp/jes/jupiter/ruby.html>.

8. The Japanese-language Proficiency Test is held both in Japan and abroad to evaluate and certify examinees' proficiency in the Japanese language. There are four levels: the criteria for each level are as follows:

   Level 1: The examinee has mastered grammar to a high level, knows about two thousand kanji and ten thousand words, and has an overall command of the language sufficient for life in Japanese society. This level provides a useful base for study at a Japanese university and is normally reached after studying Japanese for about nine hundred hours.

   Level 2: The examinee has mastered grammar to a relatively high level, knows about one thousand kanji and six thousand words, and has the ability to converse, read, and write about matters of a general nature. This level is normally reached after studying Japanese for about six hundred hours and after completing an intermediate course.

   Level 3: The examinee has mastered grammar to a limited level, knows about three hundred kanji and one thousand five hundred words and has the ability to take part in everyday conversation and read and write simple sentences. This level is normally reached after studying Japanese for around three hundred hours and after completing an elementary course.

   Level 4: The examinee has mastered the basic elements of grammar, knows around one hundred kanji and eight hundred words, and has the ability to engage in simple conversation and to read and write short, simple sentences. This level is normally reached after studying Japanese for around 150 hours and after completion of the first half of an elementary course. (Guidelines for the 1999 Japanese-Language Proficiency Test)

9. The program called VP indexes the frequency level of each word in a text. It is distributed as freeware on the Internet at <http://www.vuw.ac.nz/lals>.

10. *ChaSen* is a morphological parser developed by Matsumoto and his colleagues at the Nara Institute of Science and Technology (Matsumoto et al., 1997). It is distributed as freeware on the Internet at <http://cactus.aist-nara.ac.jp/lab/nlt/chasen.html>.

11. The text analyzed here is the first part of Lesson 1 in *Chuukyuu Nihongo,* published by Nagoya University. (See Appendix).

12. The *Kanji Counter* (Kojima and Nishina, 1997), developed at Tokyo Institute of Technology, is available on the Internet. For Japanese language education for children in Japan, there is a tool that classifies basic educational kanji (*kyouiku* kanji) according to primary school grade.

13. The VLC and the KLC are integrated into the Japanese Language Reading Tutorial System, "Reading Tutor." It contains the Dictionary Tool, Level Checker, Reading Resource Bank, Reading Tutorial Links, and Reading Comprehension Quiz. Recently we added a Japanese-German dictionary in the Reading Tutorial Toolbox (<http://language.tiu.ac.jp/tools_e.html>). We hope these will be effective tools for learners and teachers. For more details, please see Kawamura et al. (1999) or contact <kawamura@tiu.ac.jp>/ <kitamura@cs.inf.shizuoka.ac.jp>.

Appendix

Japanese Textbooks used for the Analysis

Elementary Textbooks

Bunka Gaikokugo Senmon Gakkou, ed. *Bunka Shokyuu Nihongo I and II.* Tokyo: Bunka Gaikokugo Senmon Gakkou, 1989.

Kaigai Gijutsusha Kenshuu Kyoukai. *Shin Nihongo no Kiso I and II.* Tokyo: Surii-ee-netto-waaku, 1990.

Kokusai Kouryuu Kikin Nihongo Kokusai Sentaa. *Nihongo Shoho.* Tokyo: Japan Foundation, 1981.

Intermediate Textbooks

Kokusai Kouryuu Kikin Nihongo Kokusai Sentaa. *Nihongo Chuukyuu.* Tokyo: Japan Foundation, 1996.

Nagoya Daigaku Sougou Gengo Sentaa Nihongo-ka, ed. *Gendai Nihongo Koosu Chuukyuu I and II.* Nagoya: Nagoya University, 1988 and 1990.

Tokyo Gaikokugo Daigaku Ryuugakusei Nihongo Kyouiku Sentaa. *Chuukyuu Nihongo.* Tokyo: Tokyo University of Foreign Studies, 1994.

Advanced Textbooks

Tokyo Gaikokugo Daigaku Fuzoku Nihongo Gakkou, ed. *Nihongo III.* Tokyo: Tokyo University of Foreign Studies, 1979.

References

Asakimori, T. 1994. *Maruchimedhia wo riyoushita nihongo kyouiku shien shisutemu no kaihatsu* (Development of a Computer Assisted System for Teaching and Learning Japanese using Multimedia). Tokyo: National Institute for Educational Research of Japan.

Foreign Student Education Center. 1998. *Chuujoukyuu shakai kagaku-kei dokkai kyouzai tekisuto banku* (Textbank of Reading Materials in the Social Sciences for Intermediate and Advanced Students). Tokyo: Tokyo University of Foreign Studies.

Kawamura, Y. 1998. *Dokkai no tame no reberu hantei shisutemu no kouchiku* (A Computer System for Checking the Level of Difficulty of Japanese Reading Material: Development and Uses of the Vocabulary Level Checker). *Journal of Japanese Language Education Methods* 5, no. 2:10–1.

Kawamura, Y. 1999. *Kanji no nan'ido hantei shisutemu 'Kanji Checker' wo mochiita tekisuto no bunseki* (Analysis of Japanese Textbooks using the Kanji Level Checker). *Journal of Tokyo International University* 59:73–87.

Kawamura, Y. and T. Kitamura. 1998. *Goi checker wo mochiita dokkai shien shisutemu* (A Japanese Reading Tutorial System using the Vocabulary Level Checker). *Research Report of Japan Educational Technology (JET) Research Report* 98–6: 29–34.

Kawamura, Y., K. Kaneniwa, and T. Kitamura. 1999. *Intaanetto wo katsuyoushita dokkai gakushuu shisutemu no kouchiku to sono hyouka* (Development and Evaluation of a Japanese Language Reading Tutorial System using the Internet). *Proceedings of Annual Meeting of the Society of Teaching Japanese as a Foreign Language*, Autumn, 1999: 63–8.

Kawamura, Y., T. Kitamura, and R. Hobara. 2000. *EDR Denshikajisho wo katsuyousita nihongo kyouikuyou jisho tsuuru no kaihatsu* (Development of a Reading Tutorial System for JSL and JFL Learners using the EDR Electronic Japanese-English Dictionary). *Journal of Japan Society for Educational Technology* 24 (Supplement): 7–12.

Kijima, H., and Y. Shimizu. 1998. *Dokusho shien shisutemu 'Shinsho-Library' no shikou* (A Pilot Study of Advanced Japanese Reading by the Reading Support System 'Shinsho Library': Effects of Learning and Analysis of Learning Behaviour). *Journal of Japanese Language Education Methods* 5, no. 2: 30–1.

Kitamura, T., Y. Kawamura, T. Uchiyama, M. Tara, and M. Okumura. 1999a. "CGI-DL2: The Use of Learning Process Records in a Japanese Reading Support System." In *Abstracts of the 12th World Congress of Applied Linguistics*, 367–8.

Kitamura, T., Y. Kawamura, T. Uchiyama, M. Tara, and M. Okumura. 1999b. *Gakushuu rireki kanri kinou wo motsu nihongo dokkai shien shisutemu no kaihatsu to sono hyouka* (Development and Evaluation of a Support System for Japanese Reading Comprehension with a Learning Process Management Function). *Japan Journal of Educational Technology* 23, no. 3: 127–33.

Kojima, S., and K. Nishina. 1997. *Nihongo gakushuu shien shisutemu no un'you* (Supporting System for Japanese Language Learning). *Journal of Japanese Language Education Methods* 4, no. 2: 10–11.

Matsumoto, Y., A. Kitauchi, T. Yamashita, Y. Hirano, O. Imaichi, and T. Imamura. 1997. *Nihongo keitaiso kaiseki shisutemu "ChaSen" version 1.0. Shiyou setsumei-sho* (Manual of the Japanese Language Morphological Parser "ChaSen," Version 1.0.). NAIST Technical Report. NAIST-IS-TR97007.

Nation, P. 1990. *Teaching and Learning Vocabulary*. New York: Newbury House.

Nihongo Nouryoku Shiken Kikaku Shou-i'inkai, ed. 1993. *Nihongo nouryoku shiken shutsudai kijun* (Standard of the Japanese Language Proficiency Test). Tokyo: Japan Foundation and Association of International Education.

Ochi, Y., Y. Yado, and T. Hayashi. 1997. *Denshikasareta nihongo bunsho wo kyouzai to shita kanji gakushuu shisutemu* (A Kanji Study System using Electronic Japanese Reading Materials). In *Proceedings of the 5th Joint Conference of Educational Technology*, 213–4.

Suzuki, Y. 1998. *Nihongo gakushuusha wo taishou to shita dokusho shien shisutemu no kaihatsu* (Development of a Reading Support System for Japanese Language Learners). Tokyo: International Christian University.

Tanaka, N. 1988. *Nihongo kyouiku no houhou* (Methods of Japanese Language Teaching). Tokyo: Taishuukan Shoten.

Tera, A., T. Kitamura and K. Ochimizu. 1996. *WWW burauza wo riyou-shita nihongo dokkai shien shisutemu* (Development of a Japanese Reading Support System on WWW Browser). *Journal of Japanese Language Education Methods* 3, no. 1: 10–11.

Internet-Based Self-Assessment for Language Skills

Yasu-Hiko Tohsaku and Hilofumi Yamamoto

Standards-based instruction was introduced in the United States in an effort to increase the accountability of learners and teachers and to improve learning and teaching. This trend reached foreign-language education in the early 1990s, and the National Standards for Learning Foreign Languages appeared in 1996. In standards-based instruction, assessment plays a more important role than ever for teachers as well as for learners. Standards-based instruction aims to help learners assess their own linguistic and other needs, set learning goals, improve skills, and measure whether they have achieved their learning goals. It takes time and energy for both learners and teachers to measure language skills, and it is difficult, if not impossible, to administer large-scale assessment frequently. In order to solve this problem, we developed a self-assessment system.[1]

Standards-based instruction uses the Internet for assessment processes, which makes management easy. This chapter discusses the contents, procedures, and reliability of the self-assessment system and closes with a look at future issues.

The Contents of the Self-Assessment System

Our self-assessment system evaluates language skills in terms of the rating descriptions laid out by the Interagency Language Roundtable (ILR). These descriptions were originally developed as a scale to measure the foreign language abilities of U.S. government employees. They assess four language skills, listening, speaking, reading, and writing. These skills are assessed in terms of

Level	Listening	Speaking	Reading	Writing
0	17	14	11	12
1	11	21	15	16
2	19	19	32	22
3	12	13	21	17
4				
Dummy	10	10	10	16
Total	69	77	89	

Table 5.1. Number of questions, by skill and ILR level.

six levels: from 0 to 5, or novice level to educated native speaker level. Proficiency examinations test candidates to see if they have achieved skills described for each level, and then their proficiency rating is determined. The proficiency guidelines of the American Council for the Teaching of Foreign Languages (ACTFL) are based on the ILR's rating descriptions.[2]

In our system, testees assess the four language skills, and the results determine their ILR ratings. The system includes skill questions for ILR levels 0 to 3 or above in listening, speaking and reading skills and for levels 0 to 4 in writing. The system incorporates dummy questions that do not affect the assessment of language skills.[3] Table 5.1 shows the number of question items for each skill. Some examples of skill questions for speaking follow.

Level 0
- Name basic objects around you (for example, desk, table, chair, clock).
- Give simple personal information, such as name, place of birth, and nationality.
- Talk about your likes and dislikes.

Level 1
- Ask and answer questions about specific personal experiences.
- Describe family members (appearance, profession, age, and so on).
- Ask/give information on transportation or route directions.

Level 2
- Summarize a movie that you saw.
- Describe customs and traditions of your country or the target country.
- Describe your career goals.

Level 3 and above
- State your opinions in hypothetical situations.
- Handle all sorts of business matters in a professional manner.
- Persuade people in a variety of situations (personal, professional, political negotiations, and so on).

Dummy questions
- Use all geographical dialects of the target language.
- Use all social dialects of the target language.
- Use highly specialized professional jargon.

We avoided language-specific questions, such as writing a simple letter by using hiragana, katakana, and kanji, or reading newspapers written in *hungul*, so that we can assess testees irrespective of languages.[4] For each question, testees assess themselves in terms of the following scale:

1. cannot handle at all
2. can somewhat handle, but with a lot of difficulty
3. can handle, but with some difficulty
4. can handle with little difficulty
5. can handle perfectly, with no mistake

The system presents questions randomly within each of the four skills. Testees do not know the level of skill of each question.

Internet-based Assessment Process and Procedure

Almost the entire process is executed through or on the Internet. The assessment follows the sequential procedures listed below.

1. The candidate who wishes to take a self-assessment test sends an e-mail to the system's administrator.
2. The administrator sends the candidate the web address, a user ID, and a password.
3. The candidate accesses the self-assessment web page (Figure 5.1).
4. The candidate enters the user ID and password and begins the self-assessment (Figure 5.2).
5. The candidate selects a skill for which he or she would like to self-assess (Figure 5.3).

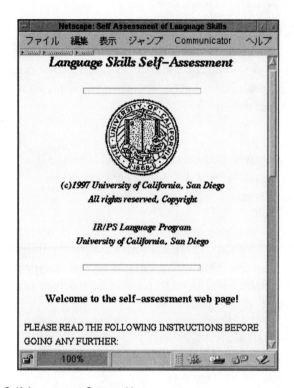

Figure 5.1. Self-Assessment Systems' home page.

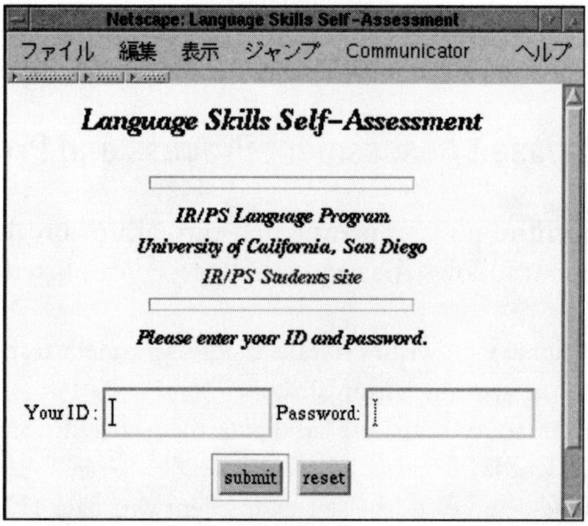

Figure 5.2. Page to enter user ID and password.

Figure 5.3. Page to select a skill.

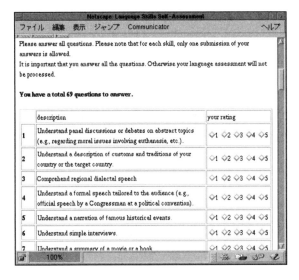

Figure 5.4. Page showing questions.

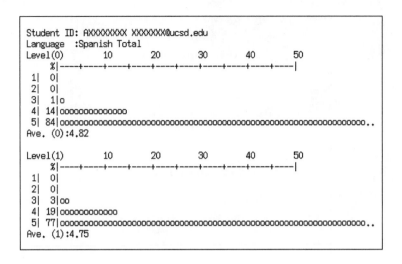

```
Student ID: AXXXXXXXX XXXXXXX@ucsd.edu
Language   :Spanish Total
Level(0)         10        20        30        40        50
     %| ----+----+----+----+----+----+----+----+----+----|
 1|   0|
 2|   0|
 3|   1|o
 4|  14|oooooooooooooo
 5|  84|ooooooooooooooooooooooooooooooooooooooooooooooooooooooooooooooooooooo..
Ave. (0):4.82

Level(1)         10        20        30        40        50
     %| ----+----+----+----+----+----+----+----+----+----|
 1|   0|
 2|   0|
 3|   3|oo
 4|  19|oooooooooooo
 5|  77|ooooooooooooooooooooooooooooooooooooooooooooooooooooooooooooooooo..
Ave. (1):4.75
```

Figure 5.5. Analytical report by e-mail.

6. A randomized list of questions appears and the candidate begins answering them (Figure 5.4).

7 The candidate finishes answering all questions for a given skill and the data goes automatically to the network server.

8 The network server transmits the data, processes and analyzes it, and then sends the analyzed data to the designated address(es) via e-mail (Figure 5.5).

9 The test administrator or teacher judges the candidate's language skills.

Reliability of the Present System

We began using the present system on an experimental basis at a graduate school in California in January 1998, and to date more than two hundred and fifty students have taken the test and assessed their language skills. By the end of July 1999, thirty-nine had taken the Foreign Service Institute's (FSI) proficiency examinations in reading and speaking.[5] Table 5.2 compares the results of self-assessment and of reading and speaking proficiency examinations.

In Table 5.2, A shows cases where self-assessment ratings and proficiency examiners' ratings are identical (for example, testees rate their speaking skill at FSI 2+, while speaking testers also rate it at FSI 2+). B shows cases in which there was a thirty per cent

	A: Perfect match		B: 33% difference		C: 66% difference	
Language	Reading	Speaking	Reading	Speaking	Reading	Speaking
Japanese	12.5(1/8)	12.5(1/8)	75.0(6/8)	75.0(6/8)	87.5(7/8)	100.0(8/8)
Chinese	12.5(1/8)	50.0(4/8)	87.5(7/8)	87.5(7/8)	100.0(8/8)	100.0(8/8)
Korean	50.0(1/2)	0.0(0/2)	100.0(2/2)	0.0(0/2)	100.0(2/2)	50.0(1/2)
Spanish	55.0(11/20)	75.0(8/12)	95.0(19/20)	95.0(19/20)	100.0(20/20)	100.0(20/20)
Vietnamese	0.0	0.0	100.0(1/1)	100.0(1/1)	100.0(1/1)	100.0(1/1)
Total	35.9(14/39)	33.3(13/39)	89.7(35/39)	84.6(33/39)	97.4(38/39)	97.4(38/39)

A: Perfect match/total number of testees
B: 33% difference/total number of testees
C: More than 66% difference/total number of testees

Table 5.2. Correspondence between self-assessment and proficiency examinations.

difference between self-assessment ratings and proficiency examiners' ratings (for example, 2+ versus 2), while C indicates cases where the difference between them is two thirds of one level (for example, 2- versus 2+).[6] A thirty per cent difference is an allowable inter-rater difference between two proficiency raters, so we can safely conclude that the present system is quite reliable, although it relies solely on testees' assessment of their own language skills.

After examining a variety of articles on self-assessment of foreign language abilities, Blanche (1988) and Blanche and Merino (1989) conclude that very able testees tend to underestimate their abilities, while less able testees overestimate them. See also Ferguson (1978), Heindler (1980) and Heilenman (1990). We could not find such a tendency in our results. Self-assessment rating and proficiency examinations seemed similar whatever the proficiency level.

According to Palmer and Backman (1981), von Elek (1981, 1982), and Anderson (1982), the areas in which testees tend to underestimate their abilities are grammar and pronunciation, whereas communicative abilities are easy to self-assess correctly. In the present system, the fact that all questions relate to communicative tasks may contribute to the accurate assessment. According to Blanche (1990), self-assessment tests thus far use questionnaires that judge language abilities based on testees' impression-based assessment of a handful of communication tasks. This tends to generate

Testee	Self-assessment	Oral proficiency examination	Difference
1	1-	1-	0
2	1-	1-	0
3	1	1	0
4	1-	1-	0
5	1-	0+	1
6	1	1-	1
7	1*	1*	0
8	1-	1	1

*Borderline case between 1 and 1+

Table 5.3. Correspondence of eight self-assessment tests and oral proficiency examinations.

overestimation. In contrast, testees in our system must assess their abilities with regard to over seventy communicative tasks. This might increase accuracy of assessment.

All testees who used our system were highly reflective master's-level graduate students taking a proficiency-based language course that focused on acquiring communicative abilities, so they practised many of the communication tasks assessed in our system.

In 1998, one Japanese government agency used our system to screen applicants for its intensive language summer program for non-native secondary-level teachers of the Japanese language. The agency wanted people with proficiency levels from FSI 1- to 1, and selected candidates based on the results of this self-test and other non-linguistic factors (such as where they were teaching). They were given an oral proficiency examination at the outset of the program. Table 5.3 compares results of the speaking self-assessment and of the oral proficiency examinations, the former compiled by an instructor at the agency who had received brief training on how to interpret graphic data such as in Figure 5.5.

With little training, language teachers familiar with, for instance, the ACTFL's proficiency guidelines and proficiency testing can determine skill ratings based on the results of our system.

Future Issues

In order to protect testees' privacy and to ensure that the results obtained by the network server are actually from the testee in question, we are currently limiting access to the system by providing a user ID and password. According to feedback from testees, it takes at least ten minutes for each of them to answer a set of questions in each skill category. We are planning to refine the system to reduce the number of questions by doing an item analysis. We hope to be able to check whether or not testees respond honestly by checking how they answered questions. The system administrator decides ratings at present, but we are developing an algorithm to allow the network server to calculate ratings automatically.

With the present system, any person who has access to the Internet and a web browser can take the test and have the results sent via e-mail to any person whom he or she designates. This "client-server computing system" is illustrated in Figure 3.1., Chapter 3 of this volume.

Students can take an examination or do a homework assignment on the Internet at any time and have the results sent automatically to the network server via the Internet. Their input can be graded, evaluated, or analyzed, and the results can be returned to them as feedback. They can also have results sent to teachers in a form that they can use for curriculum design and development, individual consultation, and research.

The system currently rates students' work on the basis of the ILR's descriptions, but with a little modification, it could use other standards or rating schemes. Such self-assessment would allow instructors

- to know in advance the approximate abilities of students transferring from other programs or schools
- to place students in an appropriate level
- to measure the development of students' abilities during a specific period
- to compare a student's abilities before and after study abroad
- to pre-test students for an advanced-level course so that they can decide what to teach

This system can be used in conjunction with other testing. Also, if we can supplement the results of this self-assessment system with data from other tests and ascertain testees' learning background, learning styles, and so forth, we will be able to measure their language skills more accurately.

In the future, we hope to provide testees themselves with feedback useful for their learning.[7]

Notes

1. Tohsaku developed the concept of this self-assessment system and
   its contents; Yamamoto, the web pages and the programming for
   collecting data and calculating and reporting the results. Language
   lecturers at the Graduate School of International Relations and
   Pacific Studies, University of California, San Diego, assisted us in
   creating assessment questions for the present system. We are grateful
   for their help and comments.
2. For reference purposes only, here are the ILR's descriptions of speaking skills for levels 1 to 4.

   Level 1
   - can satisfy routine travel needs and minimum courtesy require-
     ments
   - can ask and answer questions on very familiar topics within the
     scope of very limited language experience
   - can understand simple questions and statements, allowing for
     slowed speech, repetition, or paraphrasing
   - can express only the most elementary needs with speaking
     vocabulary
   - makes frequent errors in pronunciation and grammar, but
     speech can be understood by a native speaker accustomed to
     dealing with foreigners attempting to speak the target language

   Even though topics that are "very familiar" and elementary
   needs vary considerably among individuals, any person at Level 1
   should be able to order a simple meal, ask for shelter or lodging, ask
   and give simple directions, make purchases, and tell time.

   Level 2
   - can satisfy routine social demands and limited work require-
     ments
   - can handle with confidence, but not with facility, most social sit-
     uations, including introductions and casual conversations about
     current events, work, family, and autobiographical information
   - can handle limited work requirements, but requires help in
     handling complications or difficulties

- can follow most conversations on non-technical subjects (that is, topics that do not require specialized knowledge) and has a speaking vocabulary sufficient to express himself or herself simply with some circumlocutions
- has an intelligible accent, though faulty
- can usually handle elementary constructions accurately but without thorough or confident control of grammar

Level 3
- can speak with sufficient structural accuracy and vocabulary to participate effectively in most formal and informal conversations on practical, social, and professional topics
- can discuss particular interests and special fields of competence with reasonable ease
- has complete comprehension for a normal rate of speech
- has a broad enough vocabulary that groping for words is rare
- has an obviously foreign accent
- has sufficient control of grammar that errors do not interfere with mutual understanding and rarely disturb native speakers

Level 4
- can use language fluently and accurately on all levels normally pertinent to professional needs
- can understand and participate in any conversation within his or her range of experience with a high degree of fluency and precision of vocabulary
- is not mistaken for a native speaker
- can respond appropriately even in unfamiliar situations
- rarely errs in pronunciation and grammar
- is capable of informal interpreting from and into language

As for the "ACTFL Japanese Proficiency Guidelines," refer to ACTFL (1988).
3. We included dummy questions in order to detect whether testees respond honestly and whether responses follow any pattern.
4. Use of language-specific questions may permit collection of information on testees' linguistic abilities and needs that might help classroom teachers as well as learners. The goal of our system,

however, is to measure testees' overall linguistic level, rather than to provide teachers and learners with language-specific feedback.

5. The Foreign Service Institute's (FSI's) tests in reading and speaking proficiency involve a face-to-face interview test designed to measure reading and speaking skills in terms of the ILR's skill descriptions.

6. Among government agencies using the ILR skill descriptions, the Foreign Service Institute and the Defense Language Institute divide each level into two, for example, 0, 0+; 1, 1+; 2, 2+; and so forth for greater accuracy. The U.S. Peace Corps divides each level into three: 0-, 0, 0+; 1-, 1, 1+; we used this system in our assessment.

7. The address of the test site of our self-assessment program is available; please contact the authors: Yasu-Hiko Tohsaku <ytohsaku@ucsd.edu> and Hilofumi Yamamoto <yamagen@ucsd.edu>.

References

Achara, W. 1980. "Self-assessment in English Skills by Undergraduate and Graduate Students in Thai Universities." In *Directions in Language Testing*, edited by J. Read, 240-60. Singapore: Singapore University Press.

American Council for Teachers of Foreign Languages (ACTFL). 1988. "ACTFL Japanese Proficiency Guidelines." *Foreign Language Annals* 21, no. 4: 589–604.

Anderson, P. 1982. "Self-esteem in the Foreign Language: A Preliminary Investigation." *Foreign Language Annals* 15, no. 2: 109–14.

Barrows, T., et al. 1981. *College Students' Knowledge and Beliefs: A Survey of Global Understanding*. New Rochelle, N.Y.: Change Magazine Press.

Blanche, P. 1986. "The Relationship between Self-assessments and other Measures of Proficiency in the case of Adult Foreign Language Learners." Master's thesis, University of California, Davis.

Blanche, P. 1988. "Self-assessment of Foreign Language Skills: Implications for Teachers and Researchers." *RELC Journal* 19: 134–46.

Blanche, P. 1990. "Using Standardized Achievement and Oral Proficiency Tests for Self-assessment Purposes: The DLIFLC Study." *Language Testing* 7, no. 2: 202–29.

Blanche, P. and H. Merino. 1989. "Self Assessment of Foreign-language Skills: Implications for Teachers and Researchers." *Language Learning* 39: 313–40.

Bluc, G. 1988. "Self-assessment: The Limits of Learner Independence." *ELT Documents*: 100–18.

Ferguson, N. 1978. "Self-assessment of Listening Comprehension." *International Review of Applied Lingusitics (IRAL)* 16: 149–56.

Fok, A. 1981. *Reliability of Student Self-assessment*. Hong Kong: Hong Kong University Language Center.

Heilenman, K. 1990. "Self-assessment of Second Language Ability: The Role of Response Effects." *Language Testing* 7, no. 2: 174–201.

Heindler, D. 1980. "Teaching English in Secondary Schools: Third Project Report." Technical report. Klagenfurt, Austria: Ministry for Art and Education.

Hilton, T., J. Grandy, R. Kline, and J. Liskin-Gasparro. 1985. *Final Report: The Oral Language Proficiency of Teachers in the United States in the 1980s—An Empirical Study*. Princeton, N.J.: Educational Testing Service.

Janssen-van Dieten, A.M. 1989. "The Development of a Test of Dutch as a Second Language: The Validity of Self-assessment by Inexperienced Subjects." *Language Testing* 6: 30–46.

LeBlanc, R., and G. Painchaud. 1985. "Self-assessment as a Second Language Placement Instrument." *TESOL Quarterly* 19: 673–87.

Oller, J., and K. Perkins, eds. 1978. *Language in Education: Testing the Tests*. Rowley, Mass.: Newbury House.

Oskersson, M. 1980. *Approaches to Self-assessment in Foreign Language Learning*. Oxford: Pergamon Press.

Palmer, A. and L. Bachman. 1981. "Basic Concerns in Test Validation." *TESOL Quarterly* 16: 449–65.

Upshur, J. 1975. "Objective Evaluation of Oral Proficiency in the TESOL Classroom." In *Papers on Language Testing 1967–1974*, edited by L. Palmer and B. Spolsky. Washington, D.C.: TESOL.

von Elek, T. 1981. "Self-assessment of Swedish as a Second Language." Working paper, University of Goteborg, Goteborg, Sweden.

von Elek, T. 1982. "Test of Swedish as a Second Language: An Experiment in Self-assessment." Working paper, University of Goteborg, Goteborg, Sweden.

von Elek, T. 1985. *A Test of Swedish as a Second Language: An Experiment in Self-assessment.* Oxford: Oxford University Press.

Wesche, M., F. Morrison, D. Ready, and C. Pawley. 1990. "French Immersion: Postsecondary Consequences for Individuals and Universities." *Canadian Modern Language Review* 46, no. 3: 430-51.

Yamamoto, H. 2002. "A Gradual Approach to Technology-Based Instruction." In *Learning Japanese in the Network Society*, edited by K. Nakajima. Calgary: University of Calgary Press.

Part Three
Learner's Autonomy and Academic Language Learning

Learning through Target Language Texts

Jim Cummins

This chapter outlines the rationale underlying an approach to computer-supported language learning that uses target language text as input for learning. The text is made comprehensible to learners as a result of dictionary and learning strategy supports built into a multimedia CD-ROM design or web-based design. The dictionary supports can be provided in learners' first and second languages (L1 and L2). Learning strategy supports include graphic organizers to facilitate comprehension of content, as well as a variety of vocabulary building and grammar learning supports. These supports represent scaffolding that enables the learner/reader to process the meaning of texts that otherwise would have been inaccessible. Any text in electronic form can be imported into the system and used as authentic input for target language learning.

E-Lective Language Learning

The term *e-Lective Language Learning* is being used to label the approach. *e-Lective* is meant to signify three central aspects of the system. First, the "e-" prefix operates in a similar way to the prefix in "e-mail" to indicate that the target language text is in electronic form. Second, the text-based nature of the system is signified by the "lect" root which goes back to the Latin *legere*, "to read," with cognates in many Romance languages such as *lecture* in French, and *lectura* in Spanish, both meaning *reading*. Finally, the word "elective" signifies that learner options or choices are built into the system at many levels. For example, learners can choose which texts to read and they can self-regulate the type and degree of support they invoke while reading in the target language. The system is designed to provide the scaffolding of textual material necessary for second language learners who are being taught through the second language (e.g., ESL students) to gain access to the curriculum. It permits L2 text to serve as input for both language *learning* and language *acquisition* (Krashen, 1983).

The distinction between *learning* and *acquisition* was initially proposed by Krashen to refer to the differences between formal, intentional language learning and the informal and incidental acquisition of a language. Krashen (1983) suggested that when students are reading for meaning, they are engaged in an *acquisition* process rather than in a *learning* process. Acquisition is seen as a subconscious internalization of the semantic and structural features of the language by means of understanding messages (meaning) communicated in an authentic naturalistic context. For Krashen, this process is far more significant in promoting L2 mastery than learning, which is viewed as a conscious focus on internalizing the forms of the language through study and monitoring one's use of the language. Although Krashen's distinction has been criticized on the grounds that the criteria distinguishing *learning* from *acquisition* are difficult to define precisely in an operational manner, the theoretical status of the distinction is not at issue here. The distinction is being used simply to refer to the obvious differences between focusing on getting rapid access to meaning in the target language, as compared to studying the language with a view to internalizing its vocabulary, grammar, phonology, and discourse properties.

Premises

The e-Lective Language Learning system is based on the following premises:

1. *Virtually all applied linguists agree that access to sufficiently comprehensible input in the target language is a necessary condition for language acquisition;* most applied linguists, however, also assign a role to (a) a focus on formal features of the target language, (b) development of effective learning strategies, and (c) actual use of the target language.

2. *Formal second language teaching is relatively unsuccessful for a signifi-cant number of learners primarily as a result of impoverished input in the target language, both with respect to quality and quantity.* Consider for example, the relatively low levels of French proficiency typi-cally attained by English-speaking Canadian school-aged stu-dents, despite several years of formal study of "core French" in elementary and high school. Learners usually have minimal interaction with native-speakers of the language, and they lack the proficiency to comprehend texts in the target language that would be of interest and intellectually stimulating. Constant reference to dictionaries is cumbersome and frustrating to learners and dramatically slows the pace of reading.

3. *Target language text has the potential to provide a virtually inexhaust-ible supply of authentic comprehensible input for language learning if rapid access to meaning could be ensured.* Although this research has been largely ignored by policy-makers and practitioners, there is ample evidence that even without the supports envisaged in the proposed system, simply reading carefully chosen target lan-guage texts works better in promoting proficiency than formal teaching of the language. (See Krashen, 1993, for a review of this research.)

4. *Current computer technology can supply the necessary supports or "scaf-folds" to make a wide range of target language text comprehensible to learners, thereby fueling the language learning process.* The more learn-ers read in the target language, the more access they get to its vocabulary, grammar, idioms, etc., and the more of the language they learn.

A Sketch of the e-Lective System and its Relevance for Language Learning

The system can, in principle, be applied in any language learning context. To illustrate its application, consider an ESL high school student who has been learning English in and outside school during the two years since his or her arrival in Canada. This student will usually have acquired reasonably adequate conversational skills in English but still be far behind grade expectations in academic aspects of English (for example, reading and writing). Research has documented repeatedly that a period of between five and ten years is typically required for ESL students to catch up academically with native-speaking peers, who are also developing their English academic skills throughout their schooling (Collier, 1987; Cummins, 1981; Klesmer, 1994). For this student to catch up to grade expectations, he or she must get extensive access to the written text of the curriculum and also be supported in internalizing this language so that it can be used in his or her own writing.

The e-Lective Language Learning program is designed to support this process. The program is based on the premise that written text can serve as input for the language learning process. Furthermore, the development of academic language proficiency requires that students get extensive access to, and be enabled to harvest, the language of academic text. The low frequency and academic language vocabulary that becomes increasingly central to reading comprehension as students progress through the grades is found almost exclusively in written text.

The e-Lective System has the following major features:

- Any text in electronic form (downloaded from the Internet, scanned in, or available on CD-ROM) can be imported into the program. Thus, teachers have the opportunity to select stories and expository texts that match their students' interests and cultural backgrounds rather than relying on one-size-fits-all texts and strategies.
- Students get one-click access to L1 and English dictionary support to facilitate understanding of the meaning of individual words and sentences.
- The program 'remembers' the words that each individual student has clicked (unknown words) and provides individualized practice to students to assist them in learning this vocabulary. These practice exercises employ several varieties of receptive and productive cloze procedure and can be set at five levels of difficulty. In practice mode, immediate feedback is provided to students on the correctness of their responses. Thus, even beginning learners can experience success in understanding grade-level texts and acquiring the vocabulary of these texts.

- Students can demonstrate that they have learned previously unknown words by passing a "test" at difficulty level 3 or above (on the five-point scale). The tests employ the same cloze procedures used in Practice Mode but provide feedback only after completion of the entire test. The system tracks students' progress in transforming previously unknown words into "learned words." In this way, students are enabled to expand their academic vocabulary at their own pace and in the context of reading texts that are either relevant or intrinsically interesting to them. At the end of each month, for example, teachers can make statements such as:

José read eight texts during October containing 4,020 words. Of these, four hundred and eighty-three were originally unknown to him but, over the course of the month, he demonstrated that he had learned four hundred of these new words. The eighty-three words that José did not know and has not demonstrated knowledge of are listed below.

- At the press of a button, students can identify high frequency words, low frequency words, and academic words in the text. Academic words are the most common words that occur across different academic disciplines. Thus, different kinds of words can be targeted by the student (or teacher). If there are high frequency words that students don't know, it is particularly important to acquire these words because their general utility value is greater than that of low frequency words.
- There is also a Grammar Mode in which students, at the click of a button, can identify the different parts of speech of all the words in the text (some teacher input is necessary here to make sure the computer gets it right). If students (or their teachers) wish, they can also carry out practice exercises focused on these parts of speech. We believe that it is important to help students demystify aspects of grammar for the simple reason that knowing the functions of verbs, nouns, adjectives, and other parts of speech facilitates text comprehension and prediction of meaning.
- An environment is also provided in which students can carry out language detective work, exploring aspects of the meaning,

form, and use of different words they choose. For example, students might explore the different meanings of the English word 'cool' in advertisements. They can also research L1 equivalents of this kind of use. Or they might explore similarities and differences in the way Graeco-Latin origin words such as 'revolution' are used in Social Studies and Science; for example, they could carry out some detective work on the meanings and functions of the prefix, root, and suffix of these words.

- Finally, an environment is created to support students' creative writing in response to texts they have read. Students are encouraged to develop an orientation of critical literacy in interpreting the text. Support is provided to enable students to probe issues such as whose perspective the text is written from and whose perspectives might have been omitted from the text.

Underlying Theory

The theory underlying this system differs from (but also complements) current approaches to both conventional language teaching and multimedia design for language learning. Regardless of the emphasis in current approaches on structural versus communicative syllabus design, the starting point of both instruction and curriculum materials is *didactic*. The syllabus design of these programs incorporates predetermined language structures or functions and vocabulary that the system is designed to teach. There is usually little flexibility to accommodate the learning styles and interests of individual learners—one size fits all. By contrast, in the e-Lective system, individual learners (or teachers) can choose the material to be read according to their interests or needs, thereby increasing the likelihood of strong motivation. Learners also self-regulate the kinds of supports they invoke and the learning strategies that they themselves find useful. Access to first language dictionaries takes a matter of seconds rather than minutes, with the result that the flow of meaning is minimally interrupted. ESL students are enabled to read grade-appropriate academic content that was previously inaccessible.

Areas of Research

The e-Lective system draws on research and theory in a multitude of areas. Some of these areas are sketched below. This is followed by a review of research that directly addresses the theoretical issues underlying the approach.

1. Language learning and teaching. While there is theoretical consensus on some general issues (as noted above), there is considerable acrimony on many other issues such as the following:
   - the extent to which instruction should focus on meaning versus form.
   - the role (if any) of corrective feedback, the extent to which the first language should be used as a stepping stone to meaning or excluded as interference.
   - the role of explicit instruction in language-learning strategies.
   - the appropriate time to introduce reading and writing in the target language.
   - the age at which second language teaching should begin, and so on.
     Most of these issues become irrelevant in the proposed system because learners self-regulate the type and degree of support they desire or need.
2. Academic achievement of ESL or minority language students. Overrepresentation of minority language students in special education and drop-out statistics has been documented in many countries (Cummins, 1984) and debates about appropriate educational intervention have become highly volatile in countries such as the United States. These debates have tended to focus on the theoretical and empirical issue of the role of students' first language in learning academic skills in English. *The e-Lective system provides a means whereby English language learning students can access L2 grade appropriate curriculum and academic language at a much earlier stage than would previously have been the case, thereby reducing the risk of academic failure.*
3. Appropriate ways of teaching literacy. The public debates on "whole language" versus "phonics" approaches (and related issues) tend to obscure a vast amount of research and theory on the reading process and appropriate forms of reading and writing instruction. In the context of the rationale underlying

e-Lective, a consistent finding is that "large amounts of time for actual text reading" is the most significant predictor of reading comprehension (for example, Fielding and Pearson, 1994).

4. Critical language awareness. This area has emerged strongly in recent years as an important focus for both research and practice (for example, Andrews, 1995, and Corson, 1995, 1998). In the context of the potential of the e-Lective system, the issue becomes how to incorporate linguistic information that would encourage learners to explore the social and political functions of language use, in addition to simply its referential functions.

5. Cognitive strategy instruction. The issue of how to maximize the efficiency of learning in general has occupied cognitive psychologists since the origins of the discipline. Of particular importance for the present project are the research and theory articulated by Chamot and O'Malley (for example, 1994) and Pressley and his colleagues (1990), although there are many other researchers whose work is also relevant. *In view of the fact that text is being used as the major source of* L2 *input, it is imperative that learners make optimal use of this input by means of efficient reading and learning strategies.*

6. Computer-assisted language learning (CALL) and multimedia design. These fields are experiencing extremely rapid growth as more powerful and inexpensive computers open up new possibilities in artificial intelligence and teaching/learning. However, as Watts (1997) points out, the technology is only as powerful as the learning theory upon which the system design is based. The challenge for the present project is to design a flexible and "user-friendly" system that maximizes the learning of language and academic content within the constraints imposed by a rapidly evolving technology. As noted above, the starting point in this design process (self-regulated second-language learning using text as input) differs from most current CALL approaches, which usually set out to teach a pre-determined range of vocabulary, structures, and functions using a "one-size-fits-all" approach.

The research that relates most directly to the e-Lective rationale concerns (a) the relation between reading and language learning, and (b) the role of the student's L1, particularly student access to L1 dictionary support in L2 reading. Research on these two areas is considered below.

Reading and Language Learning

Nation and Coady (1988), in reviewing research on the relationship between vocabulary and reading, point out that "vocabulary difficulty has consistently been found to be the most significant predictor of overall readability." Once the effect of vocabulary difficulty (usually estimated by word frequency and/or familiarity and word length) is taken into account, other linguistic variables, such as sentence structure, account for little incremental variance in the readability of a text. They summarize their review as follows: "In general the research leaves us in little doubt about the importance of vocabulary knowledge for reading, and the value of reading as a means of increasing vocabulary" (p. 108). One example of the research showing the extent to which vocabulary can be acquired from context is Nagy et al. (1985), who demonstrate that the probability of learning a word from context after just one exposure is between .10 and .15. As learners read more in their second language, repeated exposure to unfamiliar words will exert an incremental effect on vocabulary learning.

The power of reading in promoting knowledge of the target language is supported in a wide variety of studies. Elley and Mangubhai (1983), for example, demonstrated that fourth and fifth grade students in Fiji exposed to a "book flood" program during their thirty-minute daily English (L2) class, in which they simply read books either alone or with the guidance of their teacher, performed significantly better after two years than students taught through more traditional methods. Elley (1991) similarly documented the superiority of book-based English language teaching programs among primary school students in a variety of other contexts.

The importance of time spent reading has also been documented in large-scale international studies of first language reading development. Postlethwaite and Ross (1992), in a large-scale international evaluation of reading achievement in thirty-two systems of education, showed that the amount of time students reported they spent in voluntary reading activities was amongst the strongest predictors (#2) of a school's overall reading performance. The first ranked indicator was the school's perception of the degree of parent co-operation, probably an index of socioeconomic status. The significance of reading frequency in promoting reading development is also evident from the high rankings of variables such as *Amount of reading materials in the school* (#8), *Having a classroom library* (#11), and *Frequency of borrowing books from a library* (#12). With respect to teaching methods, a focus on *Comprehension instruction* was ranked (#9) and *Emphasis on literature* was ranked (#17), both considerably higher than whether or not the school engaged in explicit *Phonics teaching* (#41).

Krashen (1983) has reviewed an extensive body of research demonstrating what he terms "the power of reading" for both L1 and L2 academic language development. One study (Mason and Krashen, 1997) will suffice to illustrate the typical outcome of these studies.

Working with Japanese university students of English as a foreign language (EFL), Mason and Krashen demonstrated in three experiments that extensive reading in English

> proved to be superior to traditional approaches on measures of reading comprehension, as well as on measures of writing and reading speed, and according to teacher observations, was much more popular with students. Extensive reading resulted in significantly superior gains in six out of seven comparisons for cloze and reading comprehension tests and extensive readers did better on measures of writing and reading speed. Extensive reading allowed "reluctant" students of EFL to catch up to traditional students.... (p. 101).

In a similar vein, Lightbown (1992) reported that New Brunswick elementary school students learning English as a second language through listening to tape-recorded stories and other material, while following the written text with no formal teaching, learned at least as much between grades three and six as did students in a more traditional aural-oral program. Both programs lasted for thirty minutes per day and in the experimental program, student autonomy was strictly respected insofar as there was "no teaching, no testing, no probing students' comprehension" (p. 356).

While extensive reading alone can result in significant gains in L2 vocabulary and other aspects of L2 competence, there is also evidence that focused vocabulary instruction can enhance learning. Paribakht and Wesche (1997), for example, found that university students learning English as a second language gained from both a Reading Only (RO) treatment (where they simply read target language texts and answered comprehension questions related to them) and also from a Reading Plus (RP) treatment (where they completed a variety of vocabulary exercises related to the texts in addition to reading the texts). The gains for the latter treatment were considerably greater than for the first. In addition, the researchers found that students in the Reading Plus treatment gained greater depth of vocabulary than those who just read the texts: "… many learners in the RP treatment seem to have passed the recognition level of target words and to have achieved greater depth in their knowledge of these words" (p. 189). These findings are consistent with the high ranking of Comprehension instruction in the international survey of reading achievement reported by Postlethwaite and Ross (1992).

In summary, there is overwhelming evidence that written text can serve as an important source of comprehensible input for the L2 language learning process. Furthermore, focused comprehension instruction can supplement the impact of target language reading. Paribakht and Wesche's conclusion from their study captures well the emerging consensus of the field:

> In conclusion, although reading for meaning appears to produce significant results in vocabulary acquisition, such reading supplemented with specific vocabulary exercises produces greater gains for the targeted words. This suggests that although instruction makes a difference, more focused instruction is desirable when the learning period is limited and specific vocabulary outcomes are sought. (p. 197)

Opportunities to engage in both acquisition and learning processes are incorporated into the e-Lective system. We expect that different learners will use these opportunities in different ways, according to their preferred learning strategies, previous learning experiences, and purposes for learning. Because the system is based on self-regulation, there is no need to argue for the superiority of one approach over the other in any absolute sense. Thus, the critiques of the acquisition/learning distinction are not applicable to the proposed learning approach since our use of this distinction does not entail any strong theoretical predictions, beyond the proposition that there are important differences between focusing on meaning in authentic communicative contexts and studying the formal features of the language outside of authentic communicative contexts. As suggested by the research on mastery of L2 and LI vocabulary and reading, it is desirable to incorporate opportunities for learners to engage in both acquisition and learning processes. At the same time, Krashen's emphasis on the primacy of acquisition appears justified, insofar as reading alone can produce significant gains without supplementary instruction. Instruction of components of language in isolation appears to have very limited potential for most learners.

The Role of Target Language (Monolingual) and Bilingual Dictionaries in L2 Reading

Both applied linguists and practitioners have tended to discourage students' use of bilingual dictionaries on the grounds that recourse to the LI will slow students' internalization of target language forms and appropriate usage. These views continue to reflect the widespread suspicion of the historically dominant grammar-translation method and the relatively uncritical adherence to direct method (or more recently "communicative") principles (see Stem, 1983, for reviews of these approaches). The new orthodoxy claims that the target language should be used exclusively for instructional purposes and recourse to the LI and translation should be avoided. These perspectives are evident in the following quotations:

> Poor readers lack skills in solving comprehension problems for themselves and tend to rely on 'extemal' helps, for example, word-for-word translations when reading a second language. Researchers in the field of reading research tend to agree that the practice of word-for-word translation of a second language text is of little benefit to the student. Such decoding often becomes the only strategy with which the learner approaches a second language text. As soon as the reader encounters an unknown word, the result is loss of contextual focus and overview, causing immediate frustration (Schulz, 1983). A continued reliance on word-for-word translation is not only expected to greatly interfere with the transition to direct extraction of meaning (Rivers, 1981), but will cause the reading

process to be slowed down and interrupted, thus greatly decreasing reading efficiency. (Brasche, 1991: 36)

In summary, it appears that learning vocabulary in context is widely perceived by the teaching profession as desirable, but that students either actively resist it, believing the translation condition to be superior, or fail to elaborate the strategies that might make it possible...most nonspecialist L2 learners are not dedicated linguists, and when faced with a choice between a high-effort strategy such as inferencing and a low-effort shortcut such as translation learning, they will tend to choose the latter. (Prince, 1996: 480)

Laufer and Kimmel (1997: 362) similarly summarize the research by noting the "paradox between the users' realization, on the one hand, that the monolingual dictionary is more helpful and, on the other hand, their preference for the bilingual dictionary." Their study examined the potential benefits of combining the usefulness of the monolingual dictionary with the usability of the bilingual dictionary. Both monolingual (target language) definitions and L1 dictionary equivalents were presented together and learners' look-up patterns were examined. They report that the resulting bilingualized dictionary is very effective and compatible with all types of individual preferences. They note that "learners may prefer one language for some words, the other language for other words, sometimes two languages are resorted to" (p. 368).

Two recent empirical studies compared the use of bilingual dictionaries with learning words from context. Contrary to the assumptions of many applied linguists and practitioners, dictionary use was found to result in better short-term vocabulary learning in both studies. Luppescu and Day (1993) randomly assigned 293 first year Japanese university students learning English as a foreign language to treatment and control groups. The treatment group was permitted to use their bilingual dictionaries while reading a short story. The control group was not permitted dictionary use. Subsequent vocabulary testing, immediately after reading the story, demonstrated that the students who used a dictionary scored significantly better (by about 50 per cent) than those who did not use a dictionary. The authors conclude that "this evidence strongly goes against our hypothesis that there would be no difference between the two groups, and provides support for the claim that the use of a bilingual dictionary by EFL students while reading can significantly improve indirect or incidental vocabulary reading" (p. 271). However, on the negative side, the dictionary group read the passage much more slowly than the non-dictionary group (88 words per minute versus 156 words per minute). The authors note that there was minimal correlation between time taken to read the passage and test performance, so that the superiority of the dictionary group cannot be attributed to the additional time they took to read the passage.

Prince (1996) also demonstrated the superiority of vocabulary learning under a translation condition, as compared to a contextual condition. Forty-eight university students learning English in France were presented with unknown target words either in a L2-L1 paired translation mode, or with the target words inserted into sentences. Participants were instructed to try to guess the meaning of the words from context. Both advanced and weaker learners performed significantly better under the translation condition. Weaker learners had difficulty transferring their knowledge into L2 contexts. Prince summarizes the main conclusions as follows:

> … the results of the experiment do, in fact, appear to be unequivocal as regards the main conclusions, namely (a) L2 words are easily learned when presented with their translations and (b) this is no guarantee that they will be successfully accessed for use in an L2 context (p. 488).

He suggests that alternative learning strategies that combine the advantages of the two techniques should be explored.

The researchers cited above unequivocally refute ill-conceived assumptions of some direct method/communicative advocates that the learners' L1 is a source of interference and should be banished from the instructional context, whether it is the classroom or computer. In the e-Lective system, the major problem identified with dictionary use (the time entailed in looking up works and the rupturing of learners' focus on meaning) is minimized as a result of the availability of the L1 or L2 semantic information on-line, which takes seconds rather than minutes to access a definition. Overall, in the context of the e-Lective system, these debates about the relative advantages and disadvantages of contextual learning versus learning from dictionaries are largely irrelevant. Individual learners are expected to use these supports of the e-Lective system in different ways that are consistent with their individual learning styles, previous learning experiences, and purposes for reading.

Conclusion

Most current CD-ROM programs employ a didactic approach to language learning, using multimedia to teach a predefined set of lexical, grammatical, and phonological information and skills in the target language. By contrast, the e-Lective system invites learners and their teachers to import any text in the target language that is of interest or relevance to them. The e-Lective system provides the built-in scaffolds that enable learners to gain access to the meaning of these texts and to use them as input for language learning. The self-regulated nature of the system encourages learners to use both acquisition and learning processes, broadly defined, according to their preferences. The semantic, grammatical, and phonological resources to facilitate both acquisition and learning (study) processes can be built into the system. In principle, supports for more complex aspects of critical literacy and language awareness can also be incorporated.

With respect to second language acquisition theory and research, the e-Lective approach is based on the evidence that target language text can serve as a powerful source of authentic L2 input. Thus, the more learners read in the L2, the more they get access to the semantic, grammatical, discourse, and (potentially) phonological properties of the language. However, the approach also endorses the potential usefulness for many learners of an explicit focus on both the formal properties of the target language itself and learning and reading comprehension strategies. These are not useful in isolation but only in the context both of extensive reading of target language text (which they help make comprehensible) and the learner's autonomy in choosing what linguistic or learning strategy supports are likely to be useful for him or her.

Finally, the e-Lective approach rejects direct method/communicative assumptions regarding the inadvisability of translation and L1 use in second language learning and teaching. Under appropriate conditions, bilingual dictionary use can provide rapid access to the meaning of target language text, and eliminate the frustration that is derived from attempting unsuccessfully to infer meanings from context. Similarly, thinking in the L1 and using L1 to construct the message and conceptual structure of the target language text can play a useful role in text comprehension at a deep semantic level. This tolerance and encouragement of L1 use within the system is not in any sense an argument against use of contextual cues, which should be very strongly encouraged. Nor is it an argument for translation in any absolute sense. The goal of the system is to maximize the quantity and quality of target language text processing in a wide variety of genres. Translation is both efficient and necessary for learners to gain access to the meaning of target language text that might be very much beyond their current level of competence in the language. Translation enables learners to proceed through the text, staying in the target language to the extent that their competence permits. Obviously, the rapidity of access to semantic information (in both L1 and L2) removes one of the major impediments to the efficient use of dictionaries in a non-computer environment.

In summary, research clearly needs to be carried out to assess the potential of the computer-supported language learning system described here. My intent has been to map out the theoretical assumptions of the system and its consistency with current research. The claim embedded in the paper is that the system is highly consistent with current theory and research in L2 teaching/learning, despite the fact that it departs radically from much current practice and (ill-conceived but influential) theoretical assumptions in both CALL and classroom-based L2 pedagogy.

References

Andrews, L. 1995. *Language Exploration and Awareness: A Resource Book for Teachers*. Mahwah, N.J.: Lawrence Erlbaum Associates.

Brasche, H.P. 1991. "The Design of a Computer-Mediated Reading Tool for the Enhancement of Second Language Reading Comprehension through the Provision of On-line Cues." Ph.D. diss., University of Toronto.

Chamot, Au., and M. O'Malley. 1994. *The* CALLA *Handbook: Implementing the Cognitive Academic Language Learning Approach.* Reading, Mass.: Addison-Wesley.

Collier, V.P. 1987. "Age and Rate of Acquisition of Second Language for Academic Purposes." *TESOL Quarterly* 21: 617–41.

Corson, D. 1995. *Using English Words.* Dordrecht: Kluwer Academic Publishers.

Corson, D. 1998. *Language Policy across the Curriculum.* Mahwah, N.J.: Lawrence Erlbaum Associates.

Cummins, J. 1981. "Age on Arrival and Immigrant Second Language Learning in Canada: A Reassessment," *Applied Linguistics* 2: 132–49.

Cummins, J. 1984. *Bilingualism and Special Education: Issues in Assessment and Pedagogy.* Clevedon, England: Multilingual Matters.

Cummins, J. 1996. *Negotiating Identities: Education for Empowerment in a Diverse Society.* Los Angeles: California Association for Bilingual Education.

Cummins, J. 1997. "Minority Status and Schooling in Canada." *Anthropology and Education Quarterly* 28, no. 3: 411–30.

Cummins, J. and D. Sayers. 1995. *Brave New Schools: Challenging Cultural Illiteracy through Global Learning Networks.* New York: St. Martin's Press.

Elley, W.B. 1991. "Acquiring Literacy in a Second Language: The Effect of Book-Based Programs." *Language Learning* 41: 375–411.

Elley, W.B., and F. Manghubai. 1983. "The Impact of Reading on Second Language Learning." *Reading Research Quarterly* 19: 53-67.

Fielding, L.G. and P.D. Pearson. 1994. "Reading Comprehension: What Works." *Educational Leadership* 51, no. 5: 62–8.

Klesmer, H. 1994. "Assessment and Teacher Perceptions of ESL Student Achievement." *English Quarterly* 26, no. 3: 5–7.

Krashen, S. 1983. *Principles and Practice in Second Language Acquisition.* Oxford: Pergamon Press.

Krashen, S. 1993. *The Power of Reading.* Englewood, Colo.: Libraries Unlimited.

Loufer, B., and M. Kimmel. 1997. "Bilingualised Dictionaries: How Learners Really Use Them." *System* 25: 361–69.

Lightbown, P.M. 1992. "Can They Do It Themselves? A Comprehension-Based ESL Course for Young Children." *Comprehension-Based Second Language Teaching,* edited by R. Courchene, J.J. Glidden, J. St John, and C. Therien. Ottawa: University of Ottawa Press.

Luppescu, S., and R.R. Day. 1993. "Reading, Dictionaries and Vocabulary Learning." *Language Learning* 43: 263–87.

Mason, B., and S. Krashen. 1997. "Extensive Reading in English as a Foreign Language." *System* 25: 91–102.

Nagy, W.E., P.A. Hemlan, and R.C. Anderson. 1985. "Learning Words from Context." *Reading Research Quarterly* 20, no. 2: 233–53.

Nation, P., and J. Coady. 1988. "Vocabulary and Reading." *Vocabulary and Language Teaching*, edited by R. Carter and M. McCarthy, 97–110. London: Longman.

Paribakht, T.S., and M. Wesche. 1997. "Vocabulary Enhancement Activities and Reading for Meaning in Second Language Vocabulary Acquisition." *Second Language Vocabulary Acquisition: A Rationale for Pedagogy*, edited by J. Coady and T. Huckin. Cambridge, England: Cambridge University Press.

Postlethwaite, T.N., and K.N. Ross. 1992. *Effective Schools in Reading: Implications for Educational Planners. An Exploratory Study*. The Hague: The International Association for the Evaluation of Educational Achievement.

Pressley, M., and Associates. 1990. *Cognitive Strategy Instruction that Really Improves Children's Academic Performance*. Cambridge, Mass.: Brookline Books.

Prince, P. 1996. "Second Language Vocabulary Learning: The Role of Context versus Translations as a Function of Proficiency." *The Modern Language Journal* 80: 478–493.

Rivers, W.M. 1981. *Teaching Foreign-language Skills*. Chicago: University of Chicago Press.

Schulz, R.A. 1983. "From Word to Meaning: Foreign Language Reading Instruction after the Elementary Course." *The Modern Language Journal* 67: 127–34.

Stern, H.H. 1983. *Fundamental Concepts of Language Teaching*. Oxford: Oxford University Press.

Watt, D.L.E., and H. Roessingh. 1994. "Some You Win, Most You Lose: Tracking ESL Students' Drop out in High School (1988–1993)." *English Quarterly* 26, no. 3: 5–7.

Watts, N. 1997. "A Learner-Based Design Model for Interactive Multimedia Language Learning Packages." *System* 25, no. 1: 1–8.

Audio Tapes for the Shinsho Library:
Self-Study Reading Materials

Yoko Suzuki, Hiroko Chinen Quackenbush,
and Yuri Shimizu

Generally, in Japanese-language education, students who have completed the advanced-level university course in Japanese language are considered ready for graduate-level work in Japanese. In other words, the student should have attained a nearly native-level proficiency in reading, listening comprehension, and expression, and the necessary command of grammar and sufficient vocabulary to begin research activities.

Level 1 of the Japanese Language Proficiency Test[1] requires knowledge of approximately ten thousand words. Students successful in this advanced class still have a large gap to fill in on their own, to attain the vocabulary of an average Japanese adult, who commands a vocabulary of more than forty thousand words.

An electronic book, a self-study tool called the *Shinsho Library* (Appendix A), was designed to give students extensive reading to help expand their vocabulary (Suzuki, 1999). In this study, we added audiotaped reading models to the Shinsho Library and tested them to see if they improved students' reading proficiency, including comprehension and speed. In addition, we observed students' actual learning strategies. This chapter first presents background information. Next, it examines the study itself: purpose and method, field test, results, interviews, and learning records. The chapter ends with a discussion of our findings and their significance.

Background

As background for this study, we looked at computer-based Japanese reading systems in Japan, development of the Shinsho Library, and research on the use of audio support and its effect on reading proficiency.

Japanese Reading Systems Using Computers in Japan

Computer-assisted reading systems have been developed in Japan since the late 1980s. Taji et al.'s *On Thinking of Food Problems* (1987) and Kijima's *Culture Transformation* (1990) both adapted material from university-level introductory textbooks in international relations and anthropology. Fujita (1990) proposed a "Reading Program" using the Computer Assisted System for TEaching and Learning/Japanese, CASTEL/J,[2] a Japanese-language education database. Fukada (1994), Kano (1997), Yamamoto (1995) and their research colleagues examined possible applications of the Computer Assisted TEchnical Reading System (CATERS), which is used by U.S. students learning how to read technical Japanese. Tera, Kitamura and Ochimizu (1996) developed "DictLinker," which links a Japanese-English dictionary on the Internet with an electronic Japanese text.

All these studies sought to supplement the reading of students of non-kanji-background (those whose native-language writing system does not contain kanji) by adding on-line dictionary equipment to their systems. For such students, it is extremely time-consuming to look up unfamiliar words, especially kanji, in the dictionary. They need to look up the reading in a kanji dictionary and then go to a bilingual dictionary for the meaning. The development of systems utilizing on-line dictionary searching was an attempt to greatly decrease the time spent consulting dictionaries.

Development of the Shinsho Library

The electronic book Shinsho Library contains self-study reading materials consisting of passages taken from books in the Kodansha's Gendai Shinsho series in CASTEL/J database. From the forty titles available, we chose for our study eight titles in different subjects

Lesson	Title and author	Subject and type of text	Number of pages
1	*The Dynamics of the Vertically Structured Society* by Chie Nakane	Sociology: for professionals in the field; writing style formal	8
2	*Japanese Society* by Chie Nakane	Sociology: for professionals in the field; writing style formal	16
3	*Manazashi in Human Relationships* by Tadashi Inoue	Psychology: written in plain Japanese with specific examples	21
4	*What is Yutori?* by Tsuneo Iida	Economics: written in plain Japanese with specific examples	22
5	*What Does It Mean to Work?* by Senji Kuroi	Liberal arts: aimed at students; written in plain Japanese	12
6	*Ringi and Nemawashi* by Yuichi Yamada	Liberal arts: specific examples easy to follow, but writing style otherwise formal	10
7	*Respect Language at One's Command* by Kikuo Nomoto	Language: easy reading with a lot of dialogue	35
8	*The Mysteries of Sleep* by Shojiro Inoue	Natural Science: contains limited number of technical terms	26

Table 7.1. Materials in the Shinsho Library.

to accommodate the various reading interests of the students (see Table 7.1). We extracted the beginning part of each text to form a lesson. Each lesson has between four thousand and fifteen thousand letters; the entire eight lessons contain fewer than seventy thousand letters. The proportion of kanji varies from nineteen to thirty-three per cent, and the average sentence length varies from thirty-eight to eighty-one letters.[3] The native speaker reads these passages silently in ten to fifteen minutes.

In using Shinsho Library, as the student reads from the computer screen and clicks on an unfamiliar word, a window opens to explain its meaning. About three thousand words considered difficult for students have explanations attached. Explanations usually contain: meanings explained in English or in simple Japanese; examples of word usage; related terms, such as synonyms, antonyms, co-occurrences, and derivatives; and reading of kanji (Appendix A). The program records each user's record of study (learning log), including searched words, study time, time spent on reading each page and each word explanation, student's name, and time and date of study (Appendix B).

This system has undergone several tests and modifications. Three major findings emerged from the last test (Suzuki et al., 1998; Suzuki and Shimizu, 1998). First, there were no differences in reading comprehension skills before and after the test, but reading speed increased. Second, students with a kanji background wanted to listen to the readings as they read the text on the computer screen to confirm reading of kanji, pauses, and intonation of sentences. Third, reading rates of participants (advanced-class students of Japanese) varied from fifty to four hundred letters per minute, with a mean speed of fewer than two hundred. When native Japanese students read the same text, their average speed was five hundred letters per minute. The results show a need for custom-tailored readings for kanji background students and for facilitation of faster reading by advanced-level students.

Previous Research in Audio Support

As for the effect of listening while reading, which students of kanji background thought necessary, there have been many studies of first- and second-language reading education. In the teaching of first-language reading, audio reading models for silent reading improved learners' reading comprehension and fluency (Schneeberg, 1977; Rasinski, 1990). For a second language, silent reading practice with audio reading support deepened learners' comprehension and increased their reading rates (Dhaif, 1990; Blum et al., 1995; Taguchi, 1995). Taji et al. (1987) developed a Japanese reading system using microcomputers and reported that aural reading models for silent reading raised reading speed. In the study of a multimedia system for reading Chinese, Hong (1997) reported that listening to the pronunciation of Chinese characters or phrases, by clicking on the screen, conveniently and effectively improved reading comprehension, pronunciation, and vocabulary.

These studies indicate that audio support benefits students by providing the pauses and intonations of the sentences, as well as the correct reading of kanji, and that it helps them to read at the speed of the reading models.

The Study

Purpose and Method

To provide students with audio reading support while reading, we attached audiotaped readings to the Shinsho Library as a field test. The three goals of this study were:

- to confirm the improvement of reading proficiency
- to confirm the role/benefits of audio tapes
- to observe students' learning strategy when they use this system

We assessed reading proficiency by prior- and post-tests of reading comprehension, and we recorded and compared time spent reading passages. We then surveyed the role of audio tapes in interviews following the test. We asked students if the audio tapes were useful and, if so, how. Given the results of interviews from the tests and studies prior to this study (Suzuki and Shimizu, 1998), we expected audio support to benefit students in three ways: by presenting pauses and intonations, by presenting correct reading of kanji, and by helping students to read quickly.

We surveyed learning strategies through the interviews and the students' logs that they recorded while studying. We asked the students how they used the audio tapes and how they read the Shinsho Library. We counted the total study time of each lesson, the time spent reading passages, the time spent reading searched explanations of words, and the number of words searched.

Field Test

The nineteen participants were undergraduate, graduate, or research students from private or national universities in Japan. Their language levels in Japanese were above or around the advanced level. Some had a kanji background; others did not. The tests took place in Tokyo, Nagoya, and Fukuoka, between January and April 1999.

We had audiotaped reading models of the Shinsho Library recorded on mini-discs. Two professional readers recorded the models with reading rates ranging from 230 to 290 letters per minute, which is slower than typical narrative speech in television news, 350 to 400 letters per minute.

The procedures of the field test were as follows. First, we conducted a pre-test to assess reading comprehension. The test consisted of seven short passages, followed by a multiple-choice question regarding content, and two long passages of about one thousand letters, followed by seven or eight multiple-choice questions on content (Appendix C). Second, we gave the students three weeks to use the audiotaped models to read *Respect Language at One's Command* and *Manazashi in Human Relationships* and two other lessons from the Shinsho Library. Third, a post-test assessed reading comprehension, and interviews followed the test. We recorded the reading rate in reading comprehension passages in both the pre-tests and the final tests.

Results

Table 7.2 shows the raw number and percentage of scores in the pre- and post-test for reading comprehension by pre-test score of reading.

Fifteen students increased their reading rate, and four seem to have improved their reading comprehension as well. Analysis of variance shows that there were no significant differences in the average scores of the reading comprehension in the two tests, hence no change in reading comprehension. However, reading speed increased significantly: $F(1,18) = 17.62$ ($p < .01$).

Interviews

Role of the Audio Tapes

In the interview after the field test, thirteen students responded that they benefited from listening to the audio tapes while reading on the monitor screen. We summarize the four points most frequently mentioned in their answers to the question: "What were the benefits to listening to the readings as you read?" First, they learned the reading of the kanji and sentence intonation and accent. Second, they understood the text without effort, since the pauses within the sentences were clear. Third, they read faster than when reading on their own to keep up with the speed of the tape. Fourth, they experienced increased retention of material and better concentration.

Student	Reading Comprehension (maximum 22 points)		Reading rate (letters per minute)	
	Pre	Post	Pre	Post
A	21(95%)	20(91%)	341	451 *
B	20(91%)	21(95%)	437	408
C	19(86%)	20(91%)	219	281 *
D	19(86%)	18(82%)	99	79
E	18(82%)	11(50%)	127	157 *
F	17(77%)	17(77%)	325	351 *
G	17(77%)	16(73%)	205	197
H	17(77%)	14(64%)	289	348 *
I	17(77%)	12(55%)	125	170 *
J	16(73%)	20(91%)	104	107
K	16(73%)	18(82%)	55	107 *+
L	16(73%)	17(77%)	93	161 *
M	15(68%)	10(45%)	91	129 *
N	14(64%)	10(45%)	155	168 *
O	13(59%)	17(77%)	381	430 *+
P	13(59%)	12(55%)	134	171 *
Q	13(59%)	12(55%)	142	155 *
R	10(45%)	12(55%)	61	77 *+
S	7(32%)	13(59%)	115	155 *+
Mean	15.7(71%)	15.3(69%)	184	216

Note: We assigned letters of the alphabet to each student in descending order of pre-test scores.
* Increased reading rate.
+ Increased reading comprehension (a gain of more than two points) and reading rate.

Table 7.2. Results of the pre- and post-tests.

The first three points were predicted reactions, but not the fourth point. An Arabic speaker stated: "Audio tapes are valuable, since in Arabic it is thought to be important to understand the meaning through the sounds rather than through written words."

When asked whether their normal reading or the audio tape was faster, nine out of nineteen students answered their normal reading, four said audio tape, two answered that for difficult reading material their reading was slower, and one said that both speeds were the same. The audio tapes, excluding the dialogues, ranged from 230 to 290 letters per minute. Thus thirty-five per cent of the students were reading at or under this speed.

Methods of Using Audio Tapes

When the students were asked how they were using the Shinsho Library and the mini-discs, we found that they used various methods. Each student selected methods to improve their own weak points according to the level of difficulty of the passages:

1. reading along with the audio tapes, and stopping the tape at an unfamiliar word, and looking up the meaning
2. reading through the material once without the audio tapes, looking up the meanings of unfamiliar words, then reading through the material again listening to the audio tapes
3. reading aloud along with the audio tapes
4. reading along with the audio tapes once and then looking up meanings of words while reading silently a second time
5. reading without the audio tapes and then listening to the audio tapes separately
6. listening to the audio tapes first and then reading the passages without audio tapes

These methods show the students' creativity and their use of the audio tapes as practice for listening comprehension and pronunciation exercises. Table 7.3 shows a summary of the interviews with the students.

Results of the Learning Record

Table 7.4 shows the time needed for each student to read *Manazashi in Human Relationships* and the number of words searched. Study time varied from 29 to 430 minutes. The number of searched words varied from 28 to 241. The average study time was 117 minutes, and the average number of searched words was 101.

To compare differences in usage, we selected three students according to reading speed (high, average, and low), and examined their learning logs after reading *Manazashi in Human Relationships*. Our findings were as follows (see also Table 7.5).

Student B, who had a high level in the Japanese language read 400 letters per minute and scored above 90 per cent for reading

Students	Usefulness*	Method(s)
A	0	2
B	0	1, 2
C	+	1
D	+	4
E	+	1
F	+	1, 3
G	+	1
H	+	1
I	+	1
J	+	1
K	–	1
L	+	2
M	0	1
N	+	1, 2, 3
O	0	2
P	–	1, 6
Q	+	1
R	+	1
S	+	5

* + useful; – not useful; 0 neither.

Table 7.3. Response to the interview.

comprehension. This student read through all 29 pages within about 40 minutes, consulted definitions of 45 words, and on average checked two words per page. He spent 30 minutes reading the material and eight minutes on word definitions, and he averaged about 10 seconds on each definition. The student spent from 1 to 30 seconds on a word.

Student G, of average reading speed, read about 200 letters per minute and scored 77 per cent on the reading comprehension test. She read this lesson in two sessions, each of about one hour. She took 112 minutes to read 29 pages in total, checked 3 words per page on average, and consulted the definitions of 88 words. She took approximately one hour and twenty minutes to read the material, spending less than 3 minutes per page, and she spent 33 minutes searching definitions. She spent from 2 to 59 seconds on each word.

Student D, of low reading speed, read 100 letters per minute and had a reading comprehension score of 86 per cent. He spent approximately four hours reading 12 pages, checked six or seven words per page, and consulted definitions 81 times (six of them

Students	Study time in minutes to complete (29 pages)	Number of words searched
A	124	46
B	38	45
C	n.d.	n.d.
D	430	146
E	82	104
F	79	28
G	112	88
H	113	71
I	199	77
J	133	241
K	61	43
L	85	110
M*	99	52
N	n.d.	n.d.
O	29	37
P	152	103
Q	52	127
R	96	170
S	113	226
Average	117	101

* incomplete reading (first 9 of 29 pages)
"n.d." no data (because of failure of operation)

Table 7.4. Time spent and words searched when studying *Manazashi in Human Relationships*.

Student	Study Time (mins.)	Number of pages	Number of words searched	Time spent on reading material (mins.)	Time spent on word definition (mins.)
B	38	29	45	30	8
G	112	29	88	79	33
D	240	12	75	110	125

Table 7.5. Summary of reading methods (from learning logs).

twice). The student spent about one hour and fifty minutes reading the material, or 9 minutes per page. He spent two hours and five minutes on definitions, ranging from six or seven seconds to five minutes per word. When asked about the time spent on definitions, he replied that he copied unfamiliar words into a notebook and, where the explanation was not clear, looked up the words in the dictionary in his own language. (He read the material in three sittings, totalling two and a half hours. The 29 pages on the computer screen are equivalent to 20 pages in the actual book, which is about 30 minutes of the audiotaped reading model.)

Discussion

Improvement of Reading Proficiency

In this study, we did not verify improvement of reading comprehension by students who used the Shinsho Library with audio tapes. Speed of reading increased, but this result did not guarantee greater reading comprehension. To raise students' reading ability in both comprehension and speed, we need further study on method and on materials for reading practice.

The Role of Audio Tapes

In this study, we confirmed four roles or benefits to providing audiotaped reading models for the electronic book Shinsho Library. Such a support system can:

1. present correct reading of kanji.
2. present pauses and intonations within sentences to facilitate comprehension.
3. provide speed reading training for students with slower reading.
4. facilitate concentration on comprehension.

1. Present correct reading of kanji
Most of the upper-intermediate reading classes focus on comprehension of passages. Correct reading of kanji and kanji compounds is not emphasized and is not explicitly taught. Students

learn correct readings in independent study, especially because those of kanji background can understand kanji compounds and consequently can comprehend the passages without knowing the Japanese reading of kanji. In this trial, students could easily learn the reading of kanji by listening to the audiotaped reading model. Thus, this system complements reading instruction by improving spoken Japanese, which students need for academic success.

2. Present pauses and intonation within sentences to facilitate comprehension

In spoken language, pauses and intonation convey grammatical information and facilitate grasp of meaning. Written language possesses neither dimension. An audiotaped reading model overcomes this deficiency and helps students whose grammatical weakness inhibits their comprehension.

3. Provide speed reading training

The reading rate of the audiotaped model is from 230 to 290 letters per minute. The students' silent reading rate in the pre-test was from 55 to 437 letters per minute, and, for 14 of the 19 participants, fewer than 230 (the minimum rate of the reading model). For these students, use of the reading model forces them to speed up their processing of information. For those who read intensively at a slow rate, the tape helps them to practice reading faster, and allows them to read extensively.

4. Facilitate concentration on comprehension

When students try to understand passages, they are processing information. Some stated that receiving information through two modes, auditory and visual, helps them concentrate on understanding. Processing two modes may be more difficult than processing one, but some students' experiences seemed to indicate the opposite, because the two modes complemented each other and facilitated comprehension. Consequently, the students could maintain their concentration on comprehension.

Students' Learning Strategies

Study time and strategies differed with students' ability. In order to read twenty pages from the Shinsho Library accompanied by the 30-minute audio tape, student B, who read fast, spent about 40 minutes, and the slow-reading D, more than four hours. Student B could read more than 400 letters per minute but said in the interview that the electronic book was useful in checking the reading of kanji such as 人 (person), 日 (day), and 一 (one), which have several readings. Also he found that it was easier to concentrate on reading without the audio tapes. We believe that this student no longer needs the electronic book. Student D, who spent more than four hours, read approximately 100 letters per minute. According to his interview, he was stopping the tape to listen to difficult words, copying the meanings down in a notebook, and listening to the tape again after reading along with the tape. This student was stopping the tape in the middle of reading and therefore did not realize the benefits of using the electronic book. Student D spent more time looking up meanings and hence read less material. The system was not put to good use by this student. Such students need a hard copy of the definitions and should avoid stopping in mid-reading.

In addition, some students used the Shinsho Library for pronunciation and listening comprehension practices on their own. Students who study Japanese as a foreign language in their own country have weaker listening comprehension than those who study Japanese in Japan. When the former start their academic life at universities in Japan, they find that their listening lags behind their reading. Using this system to read while listening would improve their listening ability.

Further Study

We believe that the reading comprehension practices should help students to reach the comprehension level of a native speaker when reading the material at the native speaker's speed (that is, reading at the speed at which a native speaker thinks). However, students who read less than half as quickly as native speakers (two hundred letters per minute) have proficiency far below the native speaker level and need some other aids to read and understand the contents.

Students require a large vocabulary, but reading speed is important in the early stages of learning Japanese. Even when beginners use elementary reading materials, modelling readings at natives' reading speed and providing estimated times for reading silently could be beneficial. With such assistance, the students should be able to read at the set reading speed by the end of the lesson.

This study has verified the benefits of providing audio support to the Shinsho Library. In future research, we expect to expand on this study by addressing several questions. We hope to determine the type of reading strategy that improves Japanese language skills, the type of exercises that should be added to improve reading comprehension, and how much reading and practice are necessary at various levels of Japanese language instruction.

Appendix A

Sample Screen from Shinsho Library

Menu Screen

Passage

Passage
Words with explanations are highlighted.

Word explanation
Clicking on a highlighted word brings
up its explanation in a window.

Appendix B

Learning Log (example)

学習者名 (Student Name) : xxxxxxx

/Top of History Data/ 1999年3月11日 木曜日   10:21:48 PM
001.9,0001,Home, ようこそ
012.3,0001, メニュー,Bookshelves ⎤
000.5,0001, メニュー,Bookshelves ⎥——— Menu screen
001.6,0001,MANAhyosi,Bookshelves ⎦
031.5,0001,MANAZASHI, まなざし　本文1
020.5,0001,MANADICT1, プロローグ1 - 1
038.7,0001,MANAZASHI, まなざし　本文1 ——→ Passage page 1
020.9,0009,MANADICT1, しぐさ1-9
014.4,0001,MANAZASHI, まなざし　本文1
045.9,0013,MANADICT1, 言い知れぬ1-13 ——→ Words consulted
004.8,0001,MANAZASHI, まなざし　本文1
002.0,0014,MANADICT1, 苦痛1-14
005.7,0001,MANAZASHI, まなざし　本文1
003.9,0015,MANADICT1, ともなう1-15
076.6,0001,MANAZASHI, まなざし　本文1
030.1,0019,MANADICT1, いわば1-19
002.2,0001,MANAZASHI, まなざし　本文1
057.4,0002,MANAZASHI, まなざし　本文2
041.4,0013,MANADICT2,・ のひとつにほかならない2-1 3
001.5,0002,MANAZASHI, まなざし　本文2
041.5,0003,MANAZASHI, まなざし　本文3
029.9,0006,MANADICT3, ふと3-6
 ・・・
005.5,0017,MANAZASHI, まなざし　本文17
086.2,0018,MANAZASHI, まなざし　本文18
015.3,0001, メニュー,Bookshelves
/End of History Data/ 1999年3月11日 木曜日   11:20:32 PM

Appendix C

Pre- and Post-Test of Reading Comprehension (example)

　私たちがものを考えるとき、たとえどのように考えるべきかについての知識を持っ
ていたとしても、その知識を、今ここで用いるべきだということを思いつくのは容易
ではない。とりわけ、今まで慣れ親しんだ状況と見かけの上では異なって見えるよう
な場合には、どう考えていいか途方にくれてしまったり、まったく見当違いの考え方
を適用しようとしてしまう。あるいは、本当は全然別の発想をしなければならないの
に、慣れ親しんだ状況とどこか似たところがあると、むりやりに今まで通りの考え方
を通そうとするのである。知識を持っていることと、目新しい状況の中で必要な知識
を利用できることとの間にはかなりのギャップがある。（290 letters）

（　　　　　）minutes

Sample Multiple-Choice Question for Passage A

Question 1　　このパラグラフで筆者がいいたいことは何ですか。

a.　人間は状況にしばられ、状況のなかでしか思考をはたらかせられない。

b.　人間は状況に応じて新しい知識を利用することができる。

c.　どう考えれば良いか知っていることとその知識を自由に使えることは別である。

d.　新しい状況の中で必要な知識を見つけださなければならない。

Passage B

　文章を書くにあたって、他人にわかるように書くことは大切である。しかし、やさしい文章、わかりやすい文章には味がないと考える人も、たくさんいる。これには、幾つかの理由がある。

　まず、もっとも単純な理由をあげると、<u>難解な文章に対する尊敬</u>である。私は、小・中学校の先生方の研究会に講師としてまねかれて、国語教育に関する話しをする機会をたびたびもっている。そういうとき、私はできるだけ具体的に、わかりやすく話そうと心がけているが、ときには、公演のあとで、「わかりやすい話しのなかに、むずかしい部分を含ませた方が、お話しにありがたみが増します」とか、「あまりわかりやすい話しだと、なんだ、おれたちをバカにしているのかと思われるから、ある程度はむずかしい方がよろしい」などと<u>忠告</u>を受けることがある。・・・

(1100 letters)

(　　　　　) minutes

Taken from *Bunsho Kosei Ho* by Kabashima Tadao, Kodansha Gendai Shinsho

Sample Multiple-Choice Questions for Passage B

Question 1 　「難解な文章に対する尊敬」というのはどういう気持ちですか。
a.　わかりにくい文章は、理解するのに頭を使うのでよい。
b.　わかりにくい文章がわかったときに、うれしい。
c.　わかりにくい文章は、内容のレベルが高く、理解する価値がある。
d.　わかりにくい文章は、わからなくても聞くだけで価値がある。

Question 2 　「忠告」というのは、だれがだれに「忠告」したのですか。
a.　筆者が、小・中学校の先生に。
b.　筆者が、研究会の講師に。
c.　研究会の講師が、筆者に。
d.　研究会の参加者が、筆者に。

　：
　：
　：
　：

Notes

1. *The Japanese Language Proficiency Test* (Japan Foundation and Association of International Education, Japan, 1994). For details, see note 8 in Chapter 4 of this volume.
2. CASTEL/J, a database developed by the CASTEL/J Research Group in Japan (Asakimori, 1994), contains text databases from books such as the *Kodansha Gendai Shinsho Series*, Japanese-language textbooks, Japanese-English and English-Japanese dictionaries, dictionaries of technical terms, and multimedia databases such as images of kanji writing-stroke orders, audio presentation of words, and visual illustrations of basic words. For details, see Chapter 9 of this volume.
3. We used the following linguistic-analysis programs in analyzing the data: *MCL* (Nakano, 1996) to count kanji, letters, and sentences; *Chasen* (developed by Yuji Matsumoto and his research colleagues at the Nara Institute of Science and Technology, Nara, Japan. <http://cl.aist-nara.ac.jp/>) to extract and count words; *Nihongo.bas* (developed by Hiroko San-noumaru and Sugao Ishimoto at International Christian University, Tokyo) to select fundamental words in the texts.

References

Asakimori, T. 1994. "Development of Computer Assisted System for Teaching and Learning Japanese: Japanese Language Education and Multimedia." Report submitted to the 1993 Grant-in-Aid for Scientific Research Program, Ministry of Education.

Blum, I.H., P.S. Koskinen, N. Tennant, E.M. Parker, M. Straub, and C. Curry. 1995. "Using Audiotaped Books to Extend Classroom Literacy Instruction into the Homes of Second-Language Learners." *Journal of Reading Behavior* 27, no. 4: 535–63.

Dhaif, H. 1990. "Reading Aloud for Comprehension: A Neglected Teaching Aid." *Reading in a Foreign Language* 7, no. 1: 457–64.

Fujita, M. 1990. "Reading Study Program: Problem of Developing Japanese Language Material with Selected Vocabulary and Structures." *Development of Computer Assisted Japanese Instruction System for Learners of Japanese as a Foreign Language.* Interim Report submitted to the 1989 Grant-in-Aid for Scientific Research Program, Ministry of Education, 113–48.

Fukada, A. 1994. "Methods in Technical Reading Instruction: Design and Development of a Computer-assisted Reading System." *Nihongo Kyoiku (Journal of Japanese Language Teaching)* no. 82: 13–22.

Hong, Wei. 1997. "Multimedia Computer-Assisted Reading in Business Chinese." *Foreign Language Annals* 30, no. 3: 335–44.

Horst, M., T. Cobb, and P. Meara. 1998. "Beyond a Clockwork Orange: Acquiring Second Language Vocabulary through Reading." *Reading in a Foreign Language* 11, no. 2: 207–23.

Japan Foundation and Association of International Education, Japan, eds. 1994. *Japanese Language Proficiency Test: Test Content Specifications.* Tokyo: Bonjinsha.

Kano, C. 1997. "Development of the System for Teaching and Evaluating Reading Skills in Scientific and Technical Japanese." Final Report, submitted to the 1994–96 Grant-in-Aid for International Scientific Research Program, Ministry of Education.

Kijima, H. 1990. "Selecting and Ordering Instructional Content for Academic Reading: Toward the Development of a Computer Assisted Reading System." *Proceedings of the Spring Conference, the Society for Teaching Japanese as a Foreign Language,* 85–90.

Kijima, H. and Y. Shimizu 1998. "A Pilot Study of Advanced Japanese Reading by the Reading Support System "Shinsho Library": Effects of Learning and Analysis of Learning Behavior." *Journal of Japanese Language Education Methods* 5, no. 2: 30–1.

Kijima, H., Y. Suzuki, R. Komai, Y. Kato, and H.C. Quackenbush. 1995. CAI for Advanced Japanese Reading: Development and Formative Evaluation. *Journal of Japanese Language Education Methods* 2, no. 1: 10–11.

Nakano, H. 1996. *Kokugo Gakusha no tame no Cho-Pasokon-ho, Pasokon ni yoru Nihongo Kenkyu-ho Nyumon, Goi to Moji (The Japanese Linguist's Super Computer Method, Introduction to the Research Method of Japanese Language using Personal Computer).* Tokyo: Kasama Shoten.

National Language Research Institute. 1991. *Study of Fundamental Vocabulary for Japanese Language Teaching.* Tokyo: Shuei Shuppan.

Rasinski, T. V. 1990. "Effects of Repeated Reading and Listening-while-Reading on Reading Fluency." *Journal of Educational Research* 83, no. 3: 147–50.

Schneeberg, H. 1977. "Listening while Reading: A Four Year Study." *Reading Teacher* March: 629–35.

Suzuki, Y. 1999. "The Development of a Reading Support System for Japanese Language Students." Final Report submitted by A. Oikawa to the 1998 Grant-in-Aid for Scientific Research (Specific Area of Research in Humanities and Computer), Ministry of Education. CD-ROM version.

Suzuki, Y., R. Komai, and H.C. Quackenbush. 1997. "CAI for Advanced Japanese Reading: Comprehension of the Reading Passages." *Journal of Japanese Language Education Methods* 4, no. 1: 22–23.

Suzuki, Y., H.C. Quackenbush, and H. Kijima. 1998. "The Conditions for the Effective Use of the Self-Study Reading Materials: Through the Use of the Shinsho Library." *Japan Society for Educational Technology Research Report*: 13–20.

Suzuki, Y., and Y. Shimizu. 1998. The Use and Evaluation of a Japanese Reading Support System for Foreign Students: Observations of the Special Characteristics of Chinese Students. *Proceedings of the 1998 Conference of Japan Society for Educational Technology*, 591–592.

Taguchi, E. 1997. "The Effects of Repeated Readings on the Development of Lower Identification Skills of FL Readers." *Reading in a Foreign Language* 11, no. 1: 97–119.

Taji, Y., A. Yokota, S. Ishimoto, and H. Kijima. 1987. "Developing a Learning System for Teaching Specialized Japanese by Use of Microcomputer (Advanced Level) 1: Development and Application." In H. Azuma, "A Fundamental Study on the Application of Audio Still-Picture Player to Foreign Language Learning." 1986, Report submitted to the Grant-in-Aid for Scientific Research Program, Ministry of Education, 68–104.

Tera, A., T. Kitamura, and K. Ochimizu. 1996. "Development of a Japanese Reading Support System on a www Browser." *Japanese Language Education Methods* 3, no. 1: 10–11.

Yamamoto, H. 1995. "Evaluation and Evaluation Methods of System for Reading Technical Texts." *Nihongo Kyoiku (Journal of Japanese Language Teaching)*, no. 85: 90–100.

Reading materials from Kodansha Gendai Shinsho Series:

Inoue, Tadashi. 1982. *The Manazashi in Human Relationships*. Tokyo: Kodansha.

Inoue, Shojiro. 1988. *The Mysteries of Sleep*. Tokyo: Kodansha.

Iida, Tsuneo. 1982. *What is Yutori?* Tokyo: Kodansha.

Kuroi, Senji. 1982. *What Does it Mean to Work?* Tokyo: Kodansha.

Nakane, Chie. 1967. *Japanese Society.* Tokyo: Kodansha.

Nakane, Chie. 1978. *The Dynamics of the Vertically Structured Society.* Tokyo: Kodansha.

Nomoto, Kikuo. 1987. *Respect Language at One's Command.* Tokyo: Kodansha.

Yamada, Yuichi. 1985. *Ringi and Nemawashi.* Tokyo: Kodansha.

Teaching Heritage Language: Individualized Learning

Masako O. Douglas

The pedagogical problems facing researchers and language professionals are complex. Heritage language learners display a wide range of competencies and proficiencies, which present enormous challenges in terms of designing a curriculum to accommodate individual learners. This chapter discusses effective utilization of technology for teaching heritage learners of Japanese at a university level. The discussion focuses on individualized learning, which is enabled by the technology.

In a review of the current situation of teaching heritage speakers of a language at the university level, Valdés (1995) cited the example of a course that offered Chinese for heritage students and attempted to cover in fewer instructional hours the same materials studied by the traditional foreign language learners. She argues that this approach fails to develop existing ability to more functional levels. Valdés (1995) and Valdés and Geoffrion-Vinci (1998) also question the current popular approaches. Instructors try to teach heritage language learners using principles typically applied to second or foreign language instruction. Rather than providing specialized heritage language courses, they either register students in lower level general language classes or place heritage language learners immediately in literature courses that focus on literary analysis. Valdés and Geoffrion-Vinci instead recommend further research into teaching heritage languages through interesting subject matter. Research areas that they found need immediate attention are expansion of the range of heritage language competence, transfer of literacy skills between heritage and majority languages, heritage language maintenance, and acquisition of prestige variety of the heritage language. The first three areas are relevant to the teaching of Japanese as a Heritage Language (JHL).

This chapter describes an attempt to individualize instruction, using computer technology as a main instructional tool, to accommodate Japanese heritage learners at the university level. It consists of four parts. Part I describes development of the curriculum, including: analysis of learners' needs, learner profiles, course overview, methods, objectives, and course assignments and grade assessment. Part II examines the ramifications of computer instruction in this curriculum including: the use of the Internet as an instructional tool, a new computer program that permits individualized learning and assessment of learners' progress. Part III presents the results of the learners' course evaluation. Part IV, the conclusion, examines the future direction of curriculum design.

Part I: Development of Curriculum

Needs Analysis

Our learners are in a course for heritage speakers at the University of California, Los Angeles (UCLA). (On the definition of "heritage language learners," see Valdés [1995] and Nakajima [1997].) Their competence level in basic interpersonal communication is much higher than those who have learned Japanese as a foreign language for a few years. However, in formal literacy skills and language competence, their proficiency is underdeveloped in: basic kanji and sophisticated use of kango (Chinese character compounds); in the formal register, including honorific and humble forms; and in stylistic differences, in both oral and written language.

Their language ability varies widely. Some have no knowledge of the basic kanji, which are taught at the elementary level of our program. Others possess a fairly extensive kanji vocabulary but are not competent in the formal register, which is taught at the intermediate level.

Such heritage learners take a placement test for exemption from the two-year foreign language requirement. The majority, however, cannot pass the test because of their underdeveloped skills. They need to strengthen these skills, but the existing curriculum cannot accommodate their needs.

For this reason, UCLA designed a course in intermediate Japanese for heritage learners in the spring of 1998, and it has offered the course since then.

Learner Profile

Seventeen students enrolled in the course in the spring of 1998, and fifteen in 1999. Except for two native English speakers who lived in Japan for a few years, all were heritage learners. Their knowledge of kanji varied greatly as shown by their comments:

"I did not study kanji at all."
"I learned up to the third grade in Saturday Japanese School."
"I went to Saturday Japanese School for ten years but did not study kanji well."
"I can read kanji well but cannot write them at all."

The results of the pre-test in kanji also show a wide range of ability. In order to measure the learners' kanji ability at the beginning of the course, instructors administer a kanji diagnosis test (Kano et al., 1993). The test consists of twelve parts: meaning, internal structure, shape (radicals), writing single kanji, written kanji in compounds, choice from context, usage (part of speech), usage (inflectional part), reading from context, reading single kanji (Japanese reading), reading compound kanji (Chinese reading), homophone and phonetic knowledge.

The learners' majors include: biology, business, chemistry, economics, environmental science, international relations, Japanese, linguistics, and psychology.

Course Overview

Intermediate Japanese for heritage learners is offered in the spring quarter (one quarter consists of ten weeks). It has two 1.5-hour sessions a week (Tuesday and Thursday) over ten weeks. All sessions take place in Japanese. Tuesday's sessions are used for lectures and practice, which focus on strategies for learning kanji, and on recognition and production of the formal register in oral and written language. Both heritage and non-heritage learners think that kanji are distinct and arbitrarily constructed symbols, and so they memorize them one by one repeatedly, without making any connection between them. As a result, they experience the constant frustration of rote memorization and difficulty of retention (Douglas, 1998a). They also tend to see the negative aspects of kanji, such as their complex structure, the many possible readings for a single kanji, and the endless numbers of kanji to learn. This increases their fear, anxiety, and frustration. They are not aware of the advantages of kanji, such as their compactness, their function as punctuation markers, and their built-in hints about meaning. Instructors provide strategy lessons in order to provide sufficient information about kanji and effective strategies for learning them, and to reduce the learner's fear and anxiety.

The course aims at providing learners with information about register as well as with classroom activities that expose them to it. The development of formal register is encouraged in three modes: interpersonal, interpretive, and presentational (see Standards for Foreign Language Learning in Newsletter, 1995). This is done by:

- role-playing
- situational conversation
- oral presentations
- viewing video
- listening to audio tapes
- exchanging e-mail with Japanese native speakers
- writing summaries of the articles

Videotapes of television commercials and drama, audio tapes of formal interviews and dialogues in formal settings, and Internet articles selected by the learners help them to develop formal register in oral and written language.

Thursday sessions take place in a computer lab. The first and second sessions in the course familiarize learners with the Internet and JWPce, a computer program designed to assist reading in Japanese. From the third week on, students work on their assignments individually. In class, they search for and read the materials they would like to read on the Internet and write summaries of them. Learners can obtain help from their instructor when they encounter problems in using a computer. Some still need technical support after the two sessions of a computer workshop that take place during the first two weeks. As well, students' ease of access to a computer varies. Some do not have one at home, and it is time-consuming for them to wait in line at a school lab to use a computer.

The instructor uses the sessions to provide each student with feedback on his or her learning (based on the record in their portfolio), and to administer kanji quizzes and oral interviews.

Methods

The instructor has three primary goals: to provide individualized, student-centred learning; to train students in kanji-learning strategies; and to train them to be autonomous learners. As I have already mentioned, learners' language ability, majors, and interests vary, so a standard curriculum that progresses at a uniform speed cannot accommodate everyone's needs.

The curriculum aims at training students in effective and efficient ways of learning kanji and in discovering the methods that best suit their learning styles. The current approach to teaching kanji, in which the instructor explains a handful of basic kanji and students then study the rest by themselves, needs to be re-examined. Self-study of kanji without any guidance simply encourages rote memorization, which results in negative views of kanji.

Another goal of the curriculum is to develop autonomy in the learners. A ten-week course is not enough to provide all the necessary training. Thus, the curriculum emphasizes teaching how to learn, rather than providing simple factual knowledge.

In order to achieve these goals, the instructor provides a module of the course objectives, but leaves selection of the materials and the pace of learning to the students.

Objectives

Course objectives consist of strategies, technology and communication. The theory of acquisition of second and foreign languages views strategic competence as one of the major components of language ability (Canale and Swain, 1981; Bachman, 1990; Celce-Murcia et al., 1995; Bachman and Palmer, 1996). There has been research in: learning strategies for a second language, the effect of such strategies for acquisition of second and foreign languages, and variables that affect the use of such strategies (Rubin, 1975; Bialystock, 1981; Politzer and McGroarty, 1985; Oxford, 1990; Oxford and Crookall, 1989; Oxford and Nyikos, 1989; O'Malley and Chamot, 1990). Based on the findings of a positive correlation between strategy use and language learning, this course aims at developing strategic competence. Students need to become aware of various cognitive and meta-cognitive learning strategies, and they need to employ them (or transfer them from their first language) appropriately.

According to Standards for Foreign Language Learning, objectives in Communication are grouped into the following three modes: interpersonal, interpretive, and presentational. Valdés and Geoffrion-Vinci (1998: 496) were referred to in order to obtain information about language competence of heritage learners in these three modes.

As for strategies, learners first search the Internet for reading material of interest to them. Learners also plan when to study, where, how much, and for how long. They record all such information in their portfolios to keep track of the progress of their study (meta-cognitive strategies). Second, students become aware of their weaknesses and strengths, which are assessed by a kanji diagnosis test (Kano et al., 1993) and by a kanji diagnosis test for strategy (Douglas, 1998b). Based on this information, they acquire effective methods of learning kanji. They also discover the most suitable strategies while they learn two hundred new kanji over the course (cognitive strategies). They take the same tests at the end of the course and compare the results to measure progress over the quarter.

The technology used in the course involves three elements. Students learn how to use a computer and the (new) JWPce, how to read Japanese material on the Internet, and how to send e-mail in Japanese.

Course objectives in communication fall into three categories: interpersonal, interpretive, and presentational. Each category has an oral and a written component.

In interpersonal oral language, learners exhibit growing competence in carrying out face-to-face interactions with same age and older people in culturally appropriate ways. They can exchange and discuss their opinions and individual perspectives with peers and/or speakers of Japanese on a variety of familiar topics that they learn in the course. They can also converse on unfamiliar topics, using knowledge and training from the course. Learners also develop delicate interpersonal negotiation skills such as: responding to invitations, offers, suggestions, or requests; expressing or responding to compliments and complaints; and making requests. Learners develop sensitivity to levels of formality and informality in speech.

In interpersonal written language, class members exhibit growing competence in using the written language for interpersonal communication. They can write responses in the appropriate style and register to e-mail posted by native speakers of Japanese.

As for interpreting oral texts, students display a growing ability to comprehend and interpret live and recorded texts, such as: academic lectures, narrative on television commercials, and dialogues in a formal setting. They can: identify phrases, collocations, and so forth typical of formal language and academic language use; begin to identify the tone and stance typical of formal/academic presentations in Japanese; and take notes on lecture contents.

When interpreting written texts, learners exhibit a growing competence in comprehension. They can: obtain knowledge of the organization of the Internet texts in various genres and develop interpretations of them, identify the main idea, and identify the tone and stance of various texts.

In oral presentations, students reveal increasing ability in using oral language to present information to an audience. They can present reports on assigned topics to their classmates in an appropriate style and register. They exhibit a growing capacity to monitor their speech for words, structures and expressions that are not characteristic of formal presentational language.

In making written presentations, participants show increasing competence in using written language to present information. They are able to: write summaries of the Internet texts that they read, edit their writing for common errors in grammar, and begin to edit their writing for style and register appropriate to formal written language.

Assignments	Grade (%)
Book report: Read *A Practical Guide to Learning Kanji* (Douglas, 1998a) and write a book report.	10
Read Internet articles (three newspaper articles and two others) and write a summary. Submit them by the deadline. Submit vocabulary lists and kanji worksheets as well as a work-in-progress sheet.	40
Choose one of the e-mails posted by Japanese native speakers. Read it and write a response to it.	8
Kanji quizzes (2 quizzes)	10 x 2 = 20
Oral interview	10
Presentation	5
Attendance	5
Maintenance of portfolio	2

Table 8.1. List of assignments.

Course Assignments and Assessing of Grades

Table 8.1 lists assignments and grade breakdowns. The course starts with strategy training to learn kanji. The purpose of the first assignment, a book report, is to identify kanji and kanji-learning strategies to reduce students' anxiety. This also helps them find strategies for use in the course and for continuing self-study.

The instructor asks students to find on the Japanese Internet six articles to read (three newspaper articles and two others, each of four to six paragraphs, and one e-mail message) and write a summary of each article and a response to the e-mail message. When they read articles, they make vocabulary lists and choose some of the kanji learning strategies listed in the checklist in Table 8.2 (Douglas, 1998b). This activity should make learners aware of the various strategies for learning kanji and help them choose some. Elementary learners are instructed to focus on the first five strategies, intermediate students on the rest. They should also focus on one or two strategies each time, rather than all of them at once. Each week the student submits an article, a vocabulary list, a checklist, and an updated work-in-progress sheet—a record of their progress over the course (see Table 8.3).

Checklist for your kanji learning   Name: _____

Keep this list in your portfolio, section 3. "Your work," together with your reading materials.

*Make multiple copies. You need to fill in this checklist whenever you learn kanji and make kanji worksheet.

Name: _____   Date: _____

Title of the article you read _____

The following table contains important areas, which need to be focused on when you learn kanji. When you read an article and study kanji vocabulary, decide which areas you want to focus on and start making a vocabulary list adding necessary information; for example, click "learn radicals of kanji" when your focus is on building radical knowledge. **Photocopy as a backup before you file it in your portfolio.**

Check the areas you would like to focus on when you learn kanji and make kanji worksheet.

Focal points	+
Learning meaning of each kanji, utilizing mnemonic association method and others.	
Break kanji into small parts and pay attention to familiar parts of kanji.	
Write the kanji a few times, paying attention to stroke orders.	
Pay attention to sound (yomigana) of each kanji.	
Learn radicals of kanji.	
Pay attention to similar looking kanji, which share a common component.	
Associate a new kanji with those you know.	
Learn On-yomi (Chinese reading) and Kun-yomi (Japanese reading).	
Focus on learning synonyms. Paraphrase a target word with other expressions.	
Focus on suffix and prefix. E.g. kanji which express a meaning of building (movie-theater), (class-room), (in-convenience).	
Review the compound kanji words which have the same kanji.	
Group kanji, which have the same On-reading.	
Pay attention to the component, which has the same sound.	
Pay attention to grammatical usage of the kanji:(verb) benkyoo-suru (noun) benkyoo	
Pay attention to Okurigana (inflection, which is written in hiragana).	
Learn yomigana of kanji words (not a single kanji, but a kanji compound).	
Make a sentence using the target kanji words.	

Table 8.2. Checklist to learn kanji.

Work-in-Progress Table	Name: _____

Portfolio assessment weighs 50% out of 100% final grade. This table shows assignments you should complete by the quarter end and the grade breakdown for each assignment.
Fill in the first two columns when you complete the assignment. The right four columns are for grading. I will evaluate your work and fill in the grade.
Submit this form together with your weekly assignment.
Keep these two pages in the third section of your portfolio (section 3-1).

Assignments	Date when you did the assignment	No errors 5 %	1~2 errors 4 %	3-4 errors 2%	more than 5 errors 0%
Internet article #1 Read and write summary in Japanese					
Vocab. Lists (2%)					
Kanji worksheets for the articles (1%)					
Internet article #2 Read and write summary in Japanese					
Vocab. Lists (2%)					
Kanji worksheets for the articles (1%)					
Internet article #3 Read and write summary in Japanese					
Vocab. Lists (2%)					
Kanji worksheets for the articles (1%)					
Your favorite article #1 Read and write summary in Japanese					
Vocab. Lists (2%)					
Kanji worksheets for the articles (1%)					
Your favorite article #2 Read and write summary in Japanese					
Vocab. Lists (2%)					
Kanji worksheets for the articles (1%)					
E-mail letter Vocab. Lists (2%)					
Kanji worksheets for the articles (1%)					
Write a response					
Neatness of portfolio maintenance: did student follow instructions and maintain the portfolio very well?		Yes (2%)		No (0%)	
		Total 50%			

Table 8.3. Work-in-progress record.

The learner attaches the worksheet (Table 8.3) to the summary every time he or she submits an assignment. The four columns on the right are the grade breakdown for the final submission of the summary draft. The draft can be revised as many times as the learner needs to. However, the student is to submit the first draft of each article on Thursday, so that he or she reads one new article and writes a summary of it each week. There was no weekly deadline in spring 1998, and all assignments could have been submitted any time during the ten weeks before the course ended. However, some learners did not plan their work evenly over ten weeks, which caused a final rush, resulting in unsatisfactory work. In spring 1999, therefore, submission of one assignment per week became compulsory.

For the e-mail assignment, learners read e-mail, select a message that they like, and send a reply to it. We use e-mail from the Mailing Forum of the Japanese Network (<www.JPNET.com>, which is owned by International Carrier Information Co., Recruit U.S.A. Inc.), because of its variety of topics and source countries.

Learners have one oral interview and two kanji quizzes during the course. Because they select different reading materials, the contents of the kanji quizzes differ. Since many kanji are tested—one hundred at a mid-point of the course and one hundred at the end of the course—students need to use effective ways of learning them to reinforce them regularly. The oral interview is based on classroom activities, and the format is mainly role-playing to measure the development of formal register.

Presentation focuses on articles read and on strategies of learning kanji that learners have found effective. Sharing ideas and opinions about strategies encourages learners, gives them different perspectives on kanji study, and motivates them.

Maintenance of the portfolio keeps learners aware of their progress and allows the instructor to evaluate their work. For this reason, the instructor explains the rationale for the portfolio and its format at the beginning of the course. The instructor grades its organization, however, only for a small part of the overall grade.

Part II: Ramifications of Computer Instruction

Use of the Internet as an Instructional Tool

I have found that the use of Internet materials both individualizes learning and increases actual reading time.

In traditional curriculum design, material selection is the instructor's job; all learners read the same materials at the same pace at the same time. Given heritage learners' varying language ability and profile, however, this uniform curriculum seems inappropriate. Internet materials can provide a variety of topics and levels of language difficulty. To show the wide range of learners' interests, I list below some of the articles that they chose in courses during the past two years. These articles were selected from several Japanese newspapers and from web sites searched by *Yahoo.Japan*, *Yahoo.Kids*, and the Japanese Network:

- newspaper articles: sports (trading baseball players, world records in track), entertainment (movie reviews, release of Star Wars, SMAP's PR video), politics, economics, organ transplants, "Manabungakubu" (students' course evaluation in University of Waseda), AIDS campaign, murders (shooting at a high school in Colorado), science section for children, "Juku" for preschoolers
- others: computers (description of new products), academic topics (gender in Japanese language), restaurant reviews, music ("How to cure the tone-deaf"), university course description (Sophia University)
- e-mail: reviews of the movie Godzilla, responses to a query about the United States (college tuition, the best place to live, Hollywood, good restaurants in Los Angeles, hotels in Los Angeles, telephone companies that offer discounts on long-distance calls), sports (soccer leagues, baseball player Nomo)

Students encounter two problems when they engage in reading a text printed on paper, especially in the intermediate and advanced levels which introduce more complex kanji. First, since each stroke of kanji is not clear in photocopied material, the learners cannot recognize the character easily. Second, it takes them a great deal of time to look up a character in a dictionary by radicals or by number of strokes because they have insufficient knowledge of the radicals or assume the wrong number of strokes. These problems not only frustrate them, but take up time otherwise available for reading.

Digitized materials, such as Internet material, provide solutions to these problems. Font sizes are adjustable on the screen. The printout of the text is a direct copy from the original, which tremendously enhances the quality of prints. Also, since an on-line dictionary can be used for the digitized materials, looking up takes much less time, allowing more time for actual reading. Increases in reading have been observed in other Japanese courses as well, which previously used a paper dictionary and now use an on-line dictionary.

Features of the JWPce

This section offers a brief history and introduces the functions of the JWPce, a computer program designed for our curriculum by Glen Rosenthal, a physics professor at UCLA. Rosenthal added several functions for learning kanji to the original JWP, a free shareware word processor designed by Stephen Chung. Rosenthal's original intention was to write a program that could operate on the Windows CE machine — a palm-size computer. Since the program's functions turned out to be powerful tools for learners of Japanese, the program was installed on all the computers in UCLA's computer laboratory, making it available to students. In order to run the program in a shared network, Rosenthal wrote the program for the computers on a network, and for Windows CE. It is free shareware and downloadable from the following site: <http://www.physics.ucla.edu/~grosenth/jwpce.html>.

This section introduces the following five special features of the JWPce: its on-line dictionary, its vocabulary list, its kanji information, its frequency count and its kanji search and way of marking new kanji.

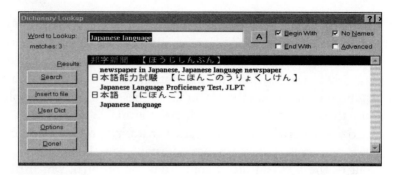

Figure 8.1a. JWPce on-line dictionary: English to Japanese

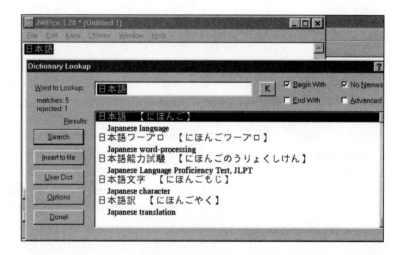

Figure 8.1b. JWPce on-line dictionary: Japanese to English

On-line dictionary

The on-line dictionary uses Jim Breen's Japanese-English dictionary. Users can look up words in both Japanese and English, as Figures 8.1a and 8.1b show.

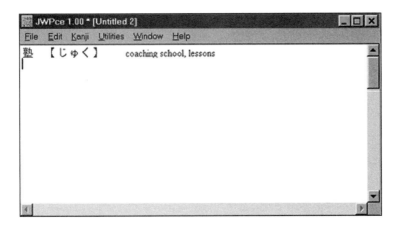

Figure 8.2. JWPce vocabulary list.

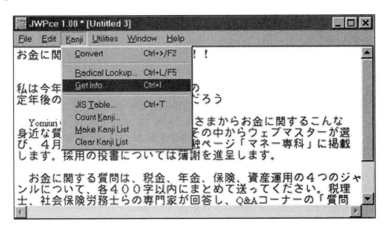

Figure 8.3a. JWPce kanji search. A: How to get kanji information.

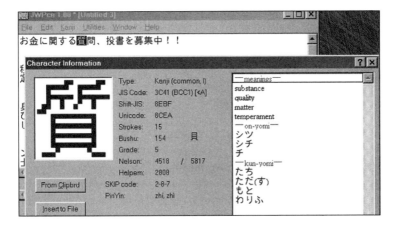

Figure 8.3b. WPce kanji search. B: Kanji information.

Vocabulary List

Learners make a vocabulary list from the reading materials they choose, using the JWPce's vocabulary list maker. The dictionary dialogue box has a button to send the target words to the vocabulary list (Figure 8.2).

Kanji Information

When students need to learn kanji, they can get information from the JWPce, as Figures 8.3a and 8.3b show. Learners click on "kanji" and then "get info" in order to obtain kanji information (Figure 8.3a). Figure 8.3b shows how kanji information is displayed.

When learners acquire kanji, they select the target two hundred from their vocabulary list according to the following two principles. First, they compare their own vocabulary list with that of the most frequent five hundred (Kano et al., 1989) or one thousand kanji (Halpern, 1993) loaded on the course web. JWPce then colours the kanji that are not on these lists.

Frequency Count

Second, they use the frequency count feature and choose the high-frequency kanji in the reading text(s). By clicking on "count," JWPce lists kanji according to the frequency. Figure 8.4. shows the kanji with the highest frequency (8) on the top of the screen, followed by kanji with lower frequency. They can check the frequency of a single text or several texts of their selection (Figure 8.4).

Kanji Search Function

Students can reinforce kanji by searching for the new target kanji in their vocabulary list. When they learn new kanji, they refer to their vocabulary lists and review the kanji that they have learned, especially the same kanji that appear repeatedly with a different combination of other kanji. The JWPce's search function makes this task easy. Learners highlight the target kanji. JWPce locates the target kanji, if it is in the learner's lists by highlighting it (Figure 8.5).

Marking New Kanji

Attrition is a problem in learning kanji. If students have no rein-
forcement, then the more they learn, the more they forget. By
selecting kanji that are common in newspapers and magazines, or
in the texts that they select and read, learners expose themselves to
the same kanji repeatedly, which reinforces them in their memory.

These features of the JWPce give learners access to the specific
information that they need. This is not possible with traditional
instructional material, such as a hard copy of the teacher's ready-
made vocabulary list or a paper dictionary.

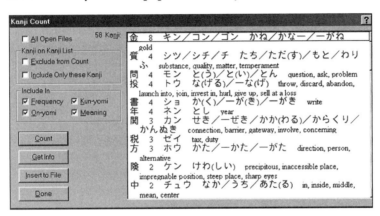

Figure 8.4. JWPce kanji frequency count.

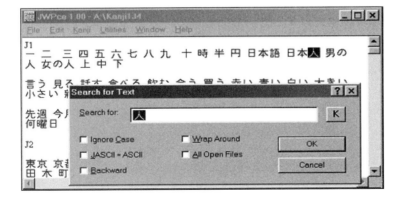

Figure 8.5. JWPce kanji search and highlighting.

Assessment of Learners' Progress

This section discusses portfolio assessment in our curriculum, which measures learners' progress and the difference in pre- and post-test results for kanji ability. The course uses the portfolio as a major assessment tool, together with the two kanji quizzes and an oral interview. Since the course aims at individualized learning, and since language ability varies widely, assessment of progress needs to be individualized. Portfolio assessment has been used in several fields: teaching of second and foreign languages (Hancock, 1994; Moya and O'Malley, 1994); assessment of elementary school children's writing (Gearhart et al., 1992); and assessment of reading (Valencia, 1990). The Center for Research on Evaluation, Standards and the Student Testing at the University of California, Los Angeles, published a large-scale project on portfolio assessment and its issues (Gearhart and Herman, 1992; National Center for Research on Evaluation, Standards & Student Testing, 1992). Office of Research (1993), Kimeldorf (1994) and Arter et al. (1995) give an overview on portfolio assessment.

Items in a portfolio vary with the purpose. For this course, a portfolio informs learners and the instructor about progress. The portfolio has three sections:

- the course syllabus and lecture notes;
- pre- and post-test results from the kanji diagnosis test and the kanji strategy test, kanji quizzes, and oral interview test results;
- all the student's work (reading material, vocabulary lists, summary drafts of texts, e-mail responses, and instructor's feedback), checklists for kanji learning, a journal, and any kanji practice sheet.

A journal is optional, but it allows an instructor to communicate with a learner, as it reflects the learner's personality and learning style.

In order to measure the effectiveness of kanji instruction, instructors administer pre- and post-tests. The results of the tests in spring 1998 appear in Table 8.4. All learners scored better in the post-test, and the difference between these two tests was statistically significant (t-test, $t = 4.43$, $df = 11$, $p < .001$). All the students significantly improved their kanji ability in ten weeks. Although the data are

Students (*n* = 12)	Pre-test raw scores (total 140)	Post-test raw scores (total 140)
1	7	19
2	21	34
3	40	50
4	45	58
5	51	56
6	58	85
7	62	75
8	81	97
9	90	102
10	93	110
11	114	122
12	116	123
Average	64.5	77.6
Standard deviation	34.7	34.5

Table 8.4. Pre- and post-test scores of kanji diagnosis test.

Questionnaire Item	Mean score
Was the Internet useful for your study?	4.7
Are you going to use the Internet in future for your study?	4.0
Did you use the on-line dictionary of the JWPce?	4.3
Did you use the colour kanji feature of the JWPce?	4.5
Did you use the frequency count of the JWPce?	2.7
Did you search kanji of the JWPce?	3.3
Did you learn formal vocabulary?	4.2
Were keigo (honorific/humble forms) lessons useful to you?	4.3

Table 8.5. Results of summative evaluation, spring 1998.

too small for any definitive conclusion, the results suggest that individualized instruction permits various, but equally effective, ways of learning. The instructor will collect more data in the course in order to examine this point in a future study.

Part III: Results of the Course Evaluation

I used formative and summative evaluation to assess the effectiveness of the program. In 1998, twelve students filled out the questionnaire. Students responded on a five-point Likert scale (1 = very low, 5 = very high); see Table 8.5.

The results show that learners highly valued the Internet as an instructional tool. They used technology (on-line dictionary and colour kanji) well in their studies. Their use of other features of the JWPce such as frequency count and search kanji, however, was low. Perhaps this was because of insufficient explanation and practice during the first two weeks of orientation. Eleven students out of twelve responded that they would continue Japanese language study by themselves, using the JWPce and the Internet. The follow-up study took place one year later. Only five learners responded, but four answered that they continued reading Japanese material on the Internet. This suggests achievement of one of the course goals, i.e., that students become autonomous learners.

To an open-ended question about the portfolio, we received the following responses (1998):

> "I could track how and what I learned by it."
> "It helped me organize my study. It is a good evaluation method."
> "It was good to have a kanji list there to refer to."
> "It forced me to work and I could see progress."

To the question about the negative aspect of the portfolio, one student answered that it was tedious.

To the other open-ended question about what students had learned from this course, they listed:

> "*Keigo* (honorific and humble forms) and a lot of vocabulary and kanji."
> "How to utilize technology, to study at my pace."
> "Studying at my pace is more efficient and accessible."

About the difficulty of the course, they responded:

> "It took time to learn the computer."
> "Kanji and *keigo* are difficult, but important."
> "Searching articles that are easy to understand was hard."

I found comments made by two students very interesting. They said that they had become confident about reading Japanese newspapers. Although newspaper articles are used very often in other advanced-level courses, none of the learners in these courses made that kind of comment. I attribute this difference to two factors. First, learners in advanced courses read clipped newspaper articles, which do not preserve the original format of the newspaper. The learners in the heritage course, by contrast, read newspaper articles on the Internet, which are not clipped, and which they find while skimming many articles. Second, an instructor selects the articles in advanced courses, while learners in heritage courses choose their own.

The articles clipped and those on the Internet are both authentic. However, there is a big difference between these two. When learners read a newspaper, they tend to skim the pages, locate articles they would like to read, and read details of the articles that they select. Reading Internet newspapers, although the format is different from the original hardcopy newspaper, provides learners with an authentic experience of reading a newspaper, which is an advantage over the clipped newspaper excerpts.

Part IV: The Future Direction of Curriculum Design

This section outlines two likely elements in the future direction of heritage language education: more study on the curriculum and potential curricular sequence.

The curriculum intends to create autonomous learners who can continue to study independently. The students' evaluations revealed that they highly valued this approach. However, its success depends on four variables: learners' access to computers, their computer skills, their different learning styles, and their attitude to self-directed learning. Further research on the feasibility of the model is needed not only in Japanese but also in other languages, such as Chinese, Spanish, and Korean, which have many heritage learners.

Information management is also a variable for the success of the program, but it imposes difficulties for both learners and instructors. The Internet is a valuable source of information. It enables learners to select reading materials of interest to them. However, as a student's comment shows, it takes learners a great deal of time to locate interesting materials that match their levels. Similarly, the amount of information on the Internet is too large for a teacher to advise his or her students. Constantly updating information on Internet material requires extra time on top of an already heavy workload.

In addition to research on the feasibility of this curriculum, we need to consider the sequence of curricula in order to develop learners' bilingual range in formal instruction. One possibility would be to offer them content-based courses in the target language to develop their academic register, which is still found underdeveloped among bilingual learners (Valdés, 1995). UCLA conducted a pilot study to implement a model called "foreign language across the curriculum" in spring 1999 (Douglas et al., 1999). It is an adjunct model for content-based instruction (Brinton, Snow and Weswche, 1989), focusing on mastery of the content, not of the language. Language instruction is supplementary. The pilot study used Introduction to Japanese linguistics, where learners on the Japanese track read fifteen per cent of reading assignments in Japanese, while those on the regular track read all their materials in English. The students' evaluation was positive, and we accordingly advocate implementation of the model in other courses. Then heritage learners with various majors and interests can take Japanese tracks in courses in their departments to expand their bilinguality.

Acknowledgments

I gratefully acknowledge Professor Chieko Kano and Mr. Jack Halpern for their generous permission to use the kanji diagnosis test and the kanji database, respectively. I am grateful to Glen Rosenthal for his design and continuous upgrading of JWPce.

References

Arter, J., et al. 1995. *Portfolio for Assessment and Instruction.* ERIC Digest. Available from ERIC Digest EDO-CG-95-10; <http://www.uncg.edu/~ericcas2'assessment/diga10.html>.

Bachman, L. 1990. *Fundamental Consideration in Language Testing.* Oxford: Oxford University Press.

Bachman, L., and A. Palmer. 1996. *Language Testing in Practice.* Oxford: Oxford University Press.

Bialystock, E. 1981. "The Role of Conscious Strategies in Second Language Proficiency." *Modern Language Journal* 65: 24–35.

Brinton, D.M., A.M. Snow, and M.B. Wesche. 1989. *Content-Based Second Language Instruction.* Boston: Heinle & Heinle Publishers.

Canale, M., and M. Swain. 1981. "A Theoretical Framework for Communicative Competence." *The Construct Validation of Tests of Communicative Competence,* edited by A. S. Palmer, P.J.M. Groot, and G.A. Trosper. Washington, D.C.: TESOL.

Celce-Murcia, M., Z. Dornyei, and S. Thurrell. 1995. "Communicative Competence: A Pedagogically Motivated Model in Content Specification." *Issues in Applied Linguistics* 6: 5–35.

Douglas, M.O. 1992. "Development of Orthography-Related Reading/ Writing Strategies by Learners of Japanese as a Foreign Language." Ph.D. diss., University of Southern California. Abstract in *Dissertation Abstracts International* 53: 3709C.

Douglas, M.O. 1998a. *A Practical Guide to Learning Kanji: For Learners from an Alphabetic Background.* San Francisco: McGraw-Hill.

Douglas, M.O. 1998b. "Strategy Inventory of Kanji Learning." Ph.D. diss., University of Southern California, revised version.

Douglas, M., S. Iwasaki, and M. Tamanaha. 1999. "Japanese across the Curriculum: A Case Study of the Model in Teaching Japanese in Advanced Level." Paper presented at a fall workshop of Teachers of Japanese in Southern California, Los Angeles, California.

Gearhart, M., J.L. Herman, E.L. Baker, and A.K. Whittaker. 1992. *Writing Portfolio at the Elementary Level: A Study of Methods for Writing Assessment.* CSE Technical Report. National Center for Research on Evaluation, Standards, and Student Testing.

Gearhart, M., J.L. Herman, E.L. Baker, and A.K. Whittaker. 1995. *Portfolio Assessment: Whose Work is It?* Center for the Study of Evaluation at the University of California, Los Angeles and the National Center for Research on Evaluation, Standards, and Student Testing. Evaluation Comment. Winter.

Halpern, J. 1993. *Frequency Data: NTC's New Japanese-English Character Dictionary.* Lincolnwood, IL: National Textbook Company.

Hancock, C.R. 1994. "Alternative Assessment and Second Language Study: What and Why?" ERIC *Clearinghouse on Languages and Linguistics.* July.

Kano, C., Y. Shimizu, H. Takanaka, and R. Ishii. 1989. *Basic Kanji Book.* Tokyo: Bonjin-sha Co.

Kano, C., Y. Shimizu, H. Takanaka, R. Ishii and T. Akutsu. 1993. *Intermediate Kanji Book: Kanji 1000 Plus.* Tokyo: Bonjin-sha Co.

Kimeldorf, M. 1994. *Portfolio Planning and Design Guide.* N.p.

Moya, S., and M.A. O'Malley. 1994. "Portfolio Assessment Model for ESL." *Journal of Educational Issues of Language Minority Students* 13: 13–36.

Nakajima, K. 1997. "Japanese as a Heritage Language: An Introduction." *Keishoogo toshiteno Nihongo Kyooiku: Kanada no Keiken o Fumaete (Japanese as a Heritage Language: The Canadian Experience)* edited by K. Nakajima and M. Suzuki, 3–20. The Canadian Association for Japanese Language Education.

National Center for Research on Evaluation, Standards and Student Testing. 1992. "Special Portfolio Issue." *Newsletter of National Center for Research on Evaluation, Standards and Student Testing.* N.p.

National Standards in Foreign Language Education. 1999. *Standards for Foreign Language Learning: Preparing for the Twenty-first Century:* National Standards in Foreign Language Education.

Office of Research, Office of Educational Research and Improvement, U.S. Department of Education. 1993. "Student Portfolio: Administrative Uses." *Consumer Guide* no. 9.

O'Malley, J.M. and A.U. Chamot. 1990. *Learning Strategies in Second Language Acquisition.* Cambridge: Cambridge University Press.

Oxford, R.L., 1990. *Language Learning Strategies.* New York: Newbury House.

Oxford, R.L., and D. Crookall. 1989. "Research on Language Learning Strategies: Methods, Findings, and Instructional issues." *Modern Language Journal* 73: 404–18.

Oxford, R.L., and M. Nyikos. 1989. "Variables Affecting Choice of Language Learning Strategies by University Students." *Modern Language Journal* 73: 291–300.

Politzer, R.L., and M. McGroarty. 1985. "An Exploratory Study of Learning Behaviors and their Relationship to Gain in Linguistic and Communicative Competence." TESOL *Quarterly* 19: 103–23.

Rubin, J. 1975. "What the Good Language Learner Can Teach Us." TESOL *Quarterly* 9: 61.

UCLA's Center for the Study of Evaluation and the National Center for Research on Evaluation, Standards, and Student Testing. 1995. Evaluation Comment. N.p.

Valencia, S. 1990. "A Portfolio Approach to Classroom Reading Assessment: The Whys, Whats, and Hows." *Reading Teacher* (January): 338–40.

Valdés, G., and M. Geoffrion-Vinci. 1998. "Chicano Spanish: The Role of the 'Underdeveloped' Code in Bilingual Repertoires." *Modern Language Journal* 70: 473–501.

Valdés, G. 1995. "The Teaching of Minority Languages as Academic Subjects: Pedagogical and Theoretical Challenges." *Modern Language Journal*, 79: 299–328.

Part Three
Collaboration and Copyright

Copyright in Japan and Distribution of the CASTEL/J Database

Akifumi Oikawa

Development of the Computer Assisted System for Teaching and Learning/Japanese (CASTEL/J) started more than ten years ago. This project aimed mainly to provide electronic materials for teaching Japanese but did not address the issue of copyright. Initial discussion among researchers at the National Institute for Educational Research in Tokyo, including the author in 1987, led to an application for a research grant (Kaken-hi: Grant-in-Aid for Scientific Research) from the Ministry of Education of Japan. The application was approved finally as a research project titled "Development of a Japanese Teaching Support System with Personal Computers for Foreigners," with chair Shigeo Miyamoto. Despite changes in personnel, the research project has continued ever since.

Two years ago, the project circulated the first CD-ROM version of the database, and currently the second version is being distributed. Already, more than two hundred discs are in the hands of domestic and foreign institutions and are being employed as teaching material, as a tool for vocabulary analysis, and so on. Development of the software for these databases is well advanced.

Many researchers use the CASTEL/J database, and insufficient understanding of the copyright issue may lead to violations of copyright. Every author possesses copyright for his or her intellectual property, and no one should violate copyright while gathering information for academic purposes.

The first section of this chapter outlines the CASTEL/J system, the second explains copyright in Japan, and the third relates Japanese copyright to CASTEL/J and its dissemination. To clarify complex issues, I quote extensively from texts on copyright, especially from *Maruchi-media to chosakuken* (Multimedia and Copyright) (Nakayama, 1996).

CASTEL/J and its Database Orientation

This section describes the CASTEL/J system and its evolution and outlines the elements of its database of teaching materials, its dictionary, and its full text databases in tabular form.

A Database-Oriented System

Initially, the CASTEL/J project was intended to develop various kinds of databases for teaching Japanese as a second/foreign language, with management software tools and application software tools for the database. While similar systems are based on software and/or hardware, CASTEL/J is database-oriented. Many other systems design functions of software before they design the structure of the database. Therefore the database depends heavily on software, and in many cases it has been difficult to use the same database on other systems.

The CASTEL/J project assumed that the database had to be appropriate for teaching Japanese with a computer. Hence its developers laid out the specifications of the database first and only later developed specifications for software to use with the database. The resulting software was independent from data and the database, and it was possible to convert the data to other systems easily.

Instructors' teaching methods, textbooks and curriculum, students' levels, and methods of learning and learning environments themselves may all differ. It is almost impossible to make a database of teaching material that suits everyone. CASTEL/J is a database that aims rather to provide the teacher and learner with enough resources as software tools so that each individual will be able to fulfill his or her needs by adapting the teaching material in appropriate ways. These resources include dictionaries, sample sentences, examination papers, the full text of paperback books, text data of play scenarios, and so on. The developers intended that CASTEL/J resources should meet the shortage of teaching materials and solve the problem of copyright in teaching Japanese in Japan and abroad.

The database of teaching material has expanded smoothly to date, but the project must address the remarkable evolution of personal computers and the rapid expansion of the Internet. The CASTEL/J project started more than ten years ago. Since then, both hardware and software have undergone a remarkable change. Many of the original programs, developed painstakingly and at much cost, became outdated with the emergence of personal computers with high performance and high function. However, many ideas that emerged in the development process survived in later software and remain as valuable assets for future development.

Many software programs today can use a browser as a common platform to read information from the Internet, which is basically software. As a result, various models of personal computers and different operating systems can use not only text but also image, voice, and animation.

The CASTEL/J project is now developing and will soon make available a program that can use a modified version of the database designed for use on the Internet. Although it is near completion, a new problem has emerged with the browser for the software to use the database. In addition, it is difficult to distribute on the Internet the various programs developed by end users who are currently using the database.

Database of Teaching Materials

The database of teaching material for CASTEL/J consists of dictionaries and full-text databases, listed in Table 9.1.

Table 9.1 lists eight types of full-text databases developed to date on CD-ROM. This includes Kodansha's two series (Gendai-shinsho Series and Blueback Series), educational material (Japanese language textbooks and proficiency tests), and others (government white papers, newspaper articles, and film scenarios). The Japan Forum and Kodansha Publications co-operated extensively in the development of the database. Kodansha gave copyright permission for use of text material for educational and academic use, which has enabled CASTEL/J to be used widely.

Dictionaries

1. **Kanji dictionary:** All 6,349 kanji characters contained in the prime and second levels of Japan Industrial Standards, or JIS,[1] appear in this dictionary. Each entry on a kanji character includes: kanji character identification number, JIS code, stroke number, radicals, *on-yomi* (Chinese phonetic reading), *kun-yomi* (Japanese semantic reading) and special reading when kanji appear in a person's name. There are three additional pieces of information: graded kanji characters taught in Japanese schools; five hundred basic kanji characters selected for beginners; and frequency according to field. Readings of each kanji character are based on *Kanwa-chu-jiten* (Kadokawa, Tokyo), a kanji dictionary considered authentic. Readings of personal names come from the "Who's Who?" directory (*Jinmei Yoran*) in the appendix of the dictionary. Each reading has two types of reading, kana and roman alphabet.

2. **Kanji-character stroke-order dictionary:** This file covers stroke order for about 3,000 kanji characters of the JIS level one, which can be easily displayed on the screen.

3. **Word dictionary:** This file is an electronic version of a dictionary *Kiso nihongo gakushu jiten* (Basic Japanese-English Dictionary), published by the Japan Foundation. It includes word identification number, kanji character index, Japanese syllabary (kana) index, roman alphabet index, frequency, etymology, parts of speech, meaning of a word in both Japanese and English, examples, related words, and antonyms.

4. **Technical glossary:** This file contains the technical words that appear in the *Monbusho gakujutu yogo-shu*, a collection of technical terms, published by the Ministry of Education in Japan. It consists of indexes (kanji and roman alphabet), English translations, and category codes such as philosophy, physics, chemistry, medicine, and so on. It contains about one hundred thousand words.

5. **Example dictionary:** Separating the dictionary of examples from that of words allows each example to be used individually, so that it may serve as an example of two or more words at the same time. About six thousand five hundred examples taken from *The Japan Foundation Basic Japanese-English Dictionary* appear in the database currently.

6. **Japanese–English dictionary:** This file has collected about thirty-three thousand index words from *The Kodansha Pax Japanese-English Dictionary* (Kodansha,1995), with readings, English translations, and so on.

7. **Pronunciation and illustration dictionary:** Some words are difficult to understand if they are given only with texts; voice information or illustrations may speed the process, especially for those who study Japanese as a second/foreign language. The CASTEL/J project, as a first step to making a multimedia database, has developed a pronunciation and a pictorial dictionary of the index words of *The Japan Foundation Basic-English Dictionary*. This dictionary has about three thousand entries.

---

1. JIS is the acronym of Japan Industrial Standards. About eight thousand standards are enacted in eighteen categories as of 1999, and each kanji is coded as a two-byte number in the category of information interchange. This standard is called "codes of the Japanese graphic character set for information interchange" and includes 6,349 kanji, grouped in two levels (Level I 2,969; Level II 3,390), according to frequency of use.

Table 9.1a. Dictionaries in CASTEL/J.

Full-Text Databases on the CD-ROM
Kodansha's Material

Gendai-shinsho Series

Aida, Yuji. *Nippon-jin no ishiki-kozo* (Structure of the Japanese Mind), 1972.
Asukai, Masamichi. *Shinsho Nihon-shi 7 / Kindai no chouryuu* (Paperback Japanese History 7/ Currents of Modern Japan), 1976.
Gouyama, Kiwamu. *Koji-seigo* (Proverbs), 1991.
Hirano, Jinkei. *Nippon no kami-gami* (Gods of Japan), 1982.
Iida, Tsuneo. *Yutori to wa nani ka* (What is a 'Composure'?), 1982.
Imazu, Akira. *Shinsho Seiyo-shi 8 / Nijusseiki no sekai* (Paperback Western History 8 / World of the 20th Century), 1974.
Inoue, Shojiro. *Suimin no fushigi* (Wonders of Sleeping), 1988.
Inoue, Tadashi. *Manazashi no ningen-kankei* (Human Relationships through Expressions of the Eyes), 1982.
Kato, Hidetoshi. *Pachinko to nippon-jin* (Pachinko and the Japanese), 1984.
Kindaichi, Haruhiko. *Nippon-jin no gengo hyogen* (Linguistic Expressions of the Japanese), 1975.
Kono, Tomomi, *Tabemono to nippon-jin* (Food and the Japanese), 1974.
Kuroi, Senji. *Hataraku to iu koto* (On Working), 1982.
Mori, Kiyoshi. *Erabi toru teinen* (On Retirement), 1992.
Morita, Yoshiyuki. *Nihongo shou-jiten /meishi hen* (Little Japanese Dictionary/Nouns), 1987.
Morita, Yoshiyuki. *Nihongo shou-jiten /doushi hen* (Little Japanese Dictionary/Verbs), 1988.
Morita, Yoshiyuki. *Nihongo shou-jiten /Keiyoushi / Fukushi hen* (Little Japanese Dictionary/ Adjectives and Adverbs), 1989.
Nakagawa, Takeshi. *Kenpo o yomu* (Reading the Constitution), 1985.
Nakagawa, Takeshi. *Nippon-jin no hou-kankaku* (The Japanese Image of the Law), 1989.
Nakane, Chie. *Tate-shakai no ningen-kankei* (Human Relations in a Vertical Society), 1967.
Nakane, Chie. *Tekiou no joken* (Conditions for Adaptation), 1972.
Nakane, Chie. *Tate-shakai no riki-gaku* (Dynamics in a Vertical Society), 1978.
Nomoto, Kikuo. *Keigo o tukai konasu* (Usage of Honorific Expressions), 1987.
Oda, Takeo. *Chizu no rekishi: Nippon* (History of Maps: Japan), 1974.
Sakurai, Tetsuo. *Tezuka Osamu* (The life of Osamu Tezuka), 1990.
Shimokawa, Koichi. *Nihon no kigyo-hatten-shi* (Development of Japanese Companies), 1990.
Takada, Hiroshi. *Essei no kaki-kata* (How to Write Essays), 1984.
Takaha, Shugyo. *Haiku no tanoshisa* (Pleasures of Haiku), 1976.
Takao, Kazuhito. *Shinsho Nihon-shi 5 / Kinsei no Nippon* (Paperback Japanese History 5/Pre-modern Japan), 1976.
Tsuduki, Takuji. *Jikan no fushigi* (Wonders of the Time), 1991.
Yamada, Yuichi. *Ringi to nemawashi* (Group-Centred Decision Making and Behind-the-Scenes Negotiations), 1985.
Yamaori, Tetsuo. *Kami to hotoke* (The God and the Buddha), 1983.
Yoshida, Jusaburo. *Koreika-shakai* (An Aging Society), 1981.
Yoshino, Hiroko. *Nippon-jin no Shisei-kan* (Death Images of the Japanese), 1982.
Yoshioka, Ikuo. *Jintai no fushigi* (Wonders of the Human Body), 1986.

Table 9.1b. Texts in CASTEL/J (1).

Blueback Series

Chiba, Yasunori. *Kioku no dai-nou-seirigaku* (Memory and Cerebral Physiology), 1991.
Nakahara, Hideomi. *Shinka-ron ga kawaru* (The Evolution Theory Will Change), 1991.
Nakamura, Mareaki. *Sake-nomi no shinrigaku* (Psychology of the Alcohol Lovers), 1990.
Nakamura, Mareaki. *Hanzai no shinrigaku* (Psychology of Crimes), 1990.
Shinagawa, Yoshiya. *Zenno-gata benkyo-ho no susume* (Introduction of a Holocerebral Way of Learning), 1987.
Yoneyama, Masanobu. *Kagaku tonchi mondo* (Quick Questions and Answers of Chemistry), 1991.

Teaching Material

School Textbooks

Atarashii shakai: chiri ni-hen (Comprehensive Social Studies: Geology Part 2) [Tokyo Shoseki Publishers Inc.].
Atarashii shakai: rekishi (Comprehensive Social Studies: History) [Tokyo Shoseki Publishers Inc.].
Atarashii shakai: koumin (Comprehensive Social Studies: The Citizen, Chapter 2) [Tokyo Shoseki Publishers Inc.].

Textbooks for Teaching Japanese as a Second Language

Japanese for You [Taishukan Publishers Inc.].

Proficiency Test

Nihongo nouryoku kentei shiken mondai (Japanese Language Proficiency Test) [The Japan Foundation].

Other Material

Government White Papers

Keizai haku-sho: Keizai kikaku-cho (Economic White Papers: Agency of Economic Planning).
Kokumin seikatsu haku-sho: Keizaikikaku-cho (White Papers of National Life: Agency of Economic Planning).
Wagakuni no bunkyou-seisaku: monbu-shou hen (Our Country's Educational Policies: Ministry of Education).

Newspapers

Selected articles from *Kita-nihon shinbun*

Film Scenarios

"*Otoko wa turai yo.*" 47 scenarios [Shouchiku Films Inc.] .

Table 9.1b. Texts in CASTEL/J (2).

Copyright in Japan

This section deals with four aspects of copyright under Japanese law: intellectual property and copyright, the definition of a "work," authors' rights, and the conditions for free legal use of a work.

Intellectual Property and Copyright

The concept of intellectual property provides the basis for copyright. The appendix to this chapter lists reports published by the Copyright Council, which are available from the Copyright Research and Information Center (CRIC) in Tokyo and form the basis for Tables 9.2–5. Nakayama (1996) explains intellectual property in *Maruchi-media to chosakuken* (Multimedia and Copyright):

> Intellectual property is information being protected from illegal copying. It is the general term that covers creative works that are the products of intellectual or spiritual endeavour (inventions, written works, and so on) and sales signs (trademarks and trade names). Intellectual property law in Japan includes patent law (for inventions), practical design law (for utility models), design law (for design), trademark law (for trademarks), SIC law (for layouts of semiconductors), seedlings law (for new varieties of vegetation), copyright law (for written works), and the law preventing unfair competition (for trademarks, business confidentiality, and commodity form). (pp. 2–3)

These laws prohibit unauthorized copying or imitation. Their aim is to protect the "value as the property of information." As the economic value of information increases and economic activities move toward being borderless, protection of information is becoming a global issue.

As a result, nations have signed international agreements such as the Paris Agreement Concerning the Protection of Industrial Property and the Berne Treaty Concerning the Protection of the Written Work. However, these documents are not sufficient in practice. Therefore discussion of enactment of international law on intellectual property is in progress in the World Intellectual Property Organization (WIPO) in the United Nations, with reform of the current treaties a likely outcome. In the meantime, GATT's Uruguay Round discussed intellectual property law, leading to a Side Trade Treaty on Rights in Intellectual Property (TRIPs) signed in 1994. A WIPO copyright agreement came into force in 1996, but Japan has not yet ratified it.

What is a "Work"?

The aim of the copyright law of Japan is specified in article 1:

> The purpose of this law is, by providing for the rights of authors and the rights neighboring thereon with respect to works as well as performances, phonograms, broadcasts, and wire diffusion, to secure the protection of the rights of authors and so on, having regard to a just and fair exploitation of these cultural products, and thereby to contribute to the development of culture.

Article 2(1)(i) defines *work* as "a production in which thoughts or sentiments are expressed in a creative way and which falls within the literary, scientific, artistic or musical domain." A work is an "expression of thoughts and sentiments," not including a collection of simple facts or data. Thus the law excludes, for example, the menu in a restaurant, the timetable of a railway station, and the telephone directory. Table 9.2 gives examples of "work" in nine categories as shown in Article 10. The copyright law also protects derivative works, edited publications, and databases (see Table 9.3). Simple data that does not have its own copyright could receive protection as an edited work if it is collected and edited in light of a certain idea.

The same is true for databases. Article 12 states:

> (1) Compilations (not falling within the term 'database'; the same shall apply hereinafter) which, by reason of the selection or arrangement of their contents, constitute intellectual creations shall be protected as independent works. (2) The provision of the preceding paragraph shall not prejudice the rights of authors of works that form part of compilations defined in that paragraph (Database works).

Article 21 states:

(1) Databases that, by reason of the selection or systematic construction of information contained therein, constitute intellectual creations shall be protected as independent works. (2) The provision of the preceding paragraph shall not prejudice the rights of authors of works that form part of databases defined in that paragraph.

The copyright law excludes the philosophy of a work from its prime subjects. Nakayama (1996) explains:

The reason why the copyright law excludes the facts or ideas (philosophy) from its prime subjects is that a big problem may occur. If the law protects ideas or philosophy apart from their expression, the protection may become very strong and may interfere with the right to express one's philosophy, or freedom of expression, or the liberty to learn, which are essential in a modern society. The law protects not facts or ideas but their expression. This reflects an international consensus. (pp. 26–7)

1	Literary Works	Thesis, novel, scenario, poetry, haiku, lecture, etc.
2	Literary Works	Music and lyrics with music.
3	Choreographic Works	Performing arts such as Japanese traditional dance, ballet, dance, etc., and pantomimes.
4	Artistic Works	Paintings, prints, sculptures, cartoons, ink calligraphy, theatre settings, etc., including ornament art.
5	Architectural Works	The building. (Design plans belong to geometrical works)
6	Maps and Figurative Works	Maps, academic drawings, charts, models, etc.
7	Cinematographic Works	Films for the cinema, television films, video programs, etc.
8	Photographic Works	Photograph, gravure, etc.
9	Computer Programs	Computer programs.

Table 9.2. Nine categories of ordinary works defined by the copyright law (ref.: C.R.I.C. homepage)

Derivative works	Translations, musical arrangements, variations and adaptations of the original work.
Edited publications	Encyclopedias, dictionaries, newspapers, magazines, anthologies, etc.
Database works	Databases.

Table 9.3. Compilations and database works protected by the copyright law (ref.: C.R.I.C. homepage)

In addition, there are works, essentially constitutional, administrative, and legal, that are not protected by the copyright law (Article 13):

> The following shall not form the subject matter of the rights provided for in this Chapter: (i) the Constitution and other laws and regulations; (ii) notifications, instructions, circular notices and the like issued by organs of the State or local public entities; (iii) judgments, decisions, orders and decrees of law courts, as well as rulings and decisions made by administrative organs in proceedings similar to judicial ones; (iv) translations and compilations of those materials mentioned in the preceding three items, made by organs of the State or local public entities.

Authors' Rights

Unlike patents and trademarks, copyright in Japan does not require pre-screening or registration in government offices. It becomes effective when a work is created. The author's rights consist of "moral rights," which protect his or her dignity as author; and "economic rights," which protect the property that he or she will earn as copyright fee. The "moral rights" are "one's exclusive rights," and only the author owns them. They cannot be transferred or be bequeathed to others. "Economic rights" protect the property. Part or all of the property may be transferred or bequeathed to others who are not the authors themselves. In Japan, copyright is valid from the date of the work's creation until fifty years after the author's death.

Works such as those that are anonymous, or are written under assumed names or a group's name, are valid for fifty years after becoming public. This time limit of fifty years commences on 1 January in the year following the author's death or the work's publication. Some countries provide for copyright protection for varying periods after the author's death; for example, Colombia, Guinea, and Panama provide eighty years; Austria, Germany, and Israel, seventy years; Brazil, sixty years; Chile, thirty years; and Cuba, twenty-five years. However, copyright disappears if the copyright owner has no heir.

Various moral and economic rights under Japanese copyright appear in Table 9.4. Moral rights govern modification, indication of authorship, and adaptation. Economic rights concern reproduction, performance, recitation, exhibition, cinematic presentation, rental, translation and adaptation, and further adaptations. But, while the author owns the copyright, others such as performers, phonogram producers, broadcasting organizations, and wire diffusion organizations, own "neighbouring rights." With neighbouring rights, the performer owns the right to record his or her performance; record manufacturers, the right to reproduce records; and broadcasting organizations, the right to record or take pictures and so on of their programs. Japanese copyright law protects all these rights.

Legal Free Use of Works

Copyright law guarantees an author's privileges. However, if the law becomes too strict, it may disturb creativity. Therefore, under certain conditions, it does allow "reasonable use" of copyrighted material such as CASTEL/J CD-ROM without obtaining permission of the copyright owner. For example, Article 33 stipulates reproduction of material in school textbooks, Article 35 reproduction in schools and other educational institutions, and Article 36 reproduction in examination papers (see Table 9.5).

Copyright and the CASTEL/J Database

As we can see in Table 9.1, a huge amount of data has been reproduced in the CASTEL/J database, such as various kinds of dictionaries and texts. We have obtained copyright permission whenever

Moral rights	
Right to control "modification"	"To offer to and to make available to the public his or her work that has not yet been made public [and] ... have the same right with respect to works derived from his or her work that has not yet been made public"
Right to control "the indication of authorship"	"To determine whether his or her true name or pseudonym should be indicated or not, as the name of the author, on the original of his or her work or when his or her work is offered to or made available to the public [and]... the same right with respect to the indication of his or her name when works derived from his or her work are offered to or made available to the public"
Right to control "change of work"	"To preserve the integrity of his or her work and its title against any distortion, mutilation, or other modification against his or her will"
Economic rights (exclusive to author)	
Reproduction	"To reproduce his or her work"
Performance	"To perform his or her work publicly ("publicly" means for the purpose of making a work seen or heard directly by the public; the same shall apply hereinafter)"
Recitation (literary work)	"To recite publicly his or her work"
Exhibition (artistic work or unpublished photographic work)	"To exhibit publicly the original of his or her work"
Cinematographic presentation	"To show his or her film and distribute (selling, lending, and so on) it to the public"
Rental	"To offer his or her work (except a cinematographic work) to the public by lending copies of the work (excluding copies of a cinematographic work in the case of a work reproduced in the cinematographic work)"
Translation and adaptation, and so on	"To translate, arrange musically or transform, or dramatize, cinematize, or otherwise adapt his or her work"
Derivative works	"In the exploitation of a derivative work, the author of the pre-existing work shall have the same rights as those the author of the derivative work has under the provisions of this subsection."

Table 9.4. Rights of authors (ref.: C.R.I.C. homepage)

Article 33 governs reproduction in school textbooks, and so on:

(1) It shall be permissible to reproduce in school textbooks ("school textbooks" means textbooks authorized by the Minister of Education or those compiled under the authorship of the Ministry of Education to be used for the education of children or pupils in primary schools, junior or senior high schools or other similar schools) works already made public, to the extent deemed necessary for the purpose of school education.
(2) A person who makes such reproduction shall inform the author thereof and pay to the copyright owner compensation, the amount of which is fixed each year by the Commissioner of the Agency for Cultural Affairs, by taking into account the purpose of the provision of the preceding paragraph, the nature and the purpose of the work, the ordinary rate of royalty, and other conditions.
(3) The Commissioner of the Agency for Cultural Affairs shall announce in the Official Gazette the amount of compensation fixed in accordance with the provision of the preceding paragraph.
(4) The provisions of the preceding three paragraphs shall apply *mutatis mutandis* with respect to the reproduction of works in textbooks intended for senior high school correspondence courses and in guidance books of school textbooks mentioned in paragraph (1) intended for teachers (these guidance books shall be limited to those published by the same publisher of the textbooks).

Article 35 covers reproduction in schools and other educational institutions: "A person who is in charge of teaching in a school or other educational institution established not for profit-making may reproduce a work already made public if and to the extent deemed necessary for the purpose of use in the course of teaching, provided that such reproduction does not unreasonably prejudice the interests of the copyright owner in the light of the nature and the purpose of the work as well as the number of copies and the form of reproduction."

Article 36 governs reproduction in examination questions: "(1) It shall be permissible to reproduce a work already made public in questions of an entrance examination or other examinations of knowledge or skill, or such examination for a licence, to the extent deemed necessary for that purpose. (2) A person who makes such reproduction for profit-making purposes shall pay to the copyright owner compensation the amount of which corresponds to an ordinary rate of royalty."

Table 9.5. Examples of permissible free use of copyright: Articles 33, 35 and 36.

necessary for any work included in CASTEL/J databases. The user can employ them without worrying about copyright, provided that his or her use is not for profit. The authors of Kodansha's Blueback series and Gendai-Shinsho series grant permission for use under the following conditions:

- The work must be used as teaching material for Japanese language education.
- The user must not reproduce the work for profit.
- The work can be made machine-readable.

- The author gives permission to use any part of his or her work.
- The user must use the copy of the work that has been produced as a CD-ROM at an organization of which the CASTEL/J Society approves.
- The author will not claim the copyright fee of the work.

As the CASTEL/J database has been developed with the generosity and support of many people, the user must make the maximum effort to respect and not to violate the copyright. We now look at unauthorized use, limits on circulation, and derivative works.

Unauthorized Use

The CD-ROM of the CASTEL/J database is currently distributed only to members of the CASTEL/J Society. There are three main reasons why this society was founded. First, the project needed a financial supporting organization besides the grants obtained from the Ministry of Education. Generally speaking, the ministry cannot guarantee a continuous grant. However, since the first grant in 1978, the project group has received generous grants continuously from the ministry under different project titles. Second, this society can apply for permission from authors to use their works in the database. Third, such an organization can easily track distribution of the CD-ROMs. It distributes CD-ROMs to members approved by the society, thereby keeping track of distribution and preventing inappropriate use. The approved member must agree not to pass a copy of the CD-ROM to a researcher or educator who is not approved as a member.

Limits on Circulation

Opening the CASTEL/J database to the public on the Internet would be appropriate, and demand is heavy. However, it is necessary to ensure strict security to prevent its illegal use. This requires money and personnel. Currently, as the society lacks the requisite resources, CASTEL/J is not available on the Internet. Therefore, users must not open its database on the Internet, even if the data is part of CASTEL/J on his or her own homepage.

Derivative Works

I predict that there will be a great deal of Japanese teaching material using the database of the CASTEL/J as users grow in number. Derivative works will emerge, such as teaching material using parts of the text database, glossaries using certain words, various kinds of dictionaries, and educational databases using some parts of the text database. Copyright in each work in CASTEL/J belongs to the author who created the work, and so the user may employ the copy of these derivative works in his or her educational organization or institution, but may not distribute these copies to others.

However, as the developers intend CASTEL/J to be shared widely as a resource, they hope that the derivative works will also be shared widely. It might be very difficult for the user to obtain permission from each author, although it is necessary to do so. Therefore the developers hope that the society will take on the task of obtaining permission from the authors on behalf of the user, even in regard to derivative works. This task is important for the future development of CASTEL/J.

Conclusion

Whether CASTEL/J can support the teaching of Japanese depends on how the individual users employ the database contained on the single disc of the CD-ROM. In the past, much effort has been made to enrich its content. But priority in software development will go to how effectively the database could be used. Currently, a group of researchers of the National Institute for Educational Research, together with their collaborators, is developing search engine software for the Internet browser. We hope that software that users develop based on the CASTEL/J database will be widely distributed through CASTEL/J.

References

Copyright Research and Information Center. 1998. *Chosakuken horei-shu (Rules and Regulations of Copyright)*. 1998. Tokyo.

Kadokawa Shoten. 1983. *Kanwa-chu-jiten* (Kanji Dictionary). Tokyo.

Nakayama, N. 1996. *Maruchi-media to chosakuken* (Multimedia and Copyright). Iwanami-shinsho no. 426. Tokyo: Iwanami Shoten.

Okamoto, K., K. Nawa, and A. Mino. 1998. *Tettei toron ittai dare no tame no chosakuken?* (Controversy on Copyright). *Hon to Conpyuutaa* (Books and Computers) 5, 93-107.

The Japan Foundation. 1986. *The Japan Foundation Kiso Nihongo Gakushu Jiten* (Basic Japanese-English Dictionary). Tokyo.

Kodansha. 1995. *The Kodansha Pax Japanese-English Dictionary*. Tokyo.

Reference homepages

Ueno, H. <http://ha1.seikyou.ne.jp/home/ueno/>

Copyright Research and Information Center. <http://www.cric.or.jp/>

Agency for Cultural Affairs. <http://www.bunka.go.jp/>

Appendix: Reports of Copyright Council

For Reports of the Copyright Council, see the important dates that follow. These reports are available from the homepage of the Copyright Research and Information Center, Tokyo, at <http://www.cric.or.jp/>.

June 1973	Second Subcommittee. Report on Computers.
September 1976	Fourth Subcommittee. Report on Reproductions and Photocopying.
January 1984	Sixth Subcommittee. Report on Computer Software.
November 1993	Ninth Subcommittee. Report on Creative Works Produced with Computers.
April 1984	Research Collaborator's Committee. Report on the Centralized Management of Copyrights.

September 1985	Seventh Subcommittee. Report on Databases and New Media.
November 1993	The Multimedia Subcommittee. First Report.
May 1994	Research Collaborator's Committee Report on Computer Programming.
February 1995	The Multimedia Subcommittee Working Group. Report of the Working Process.
February 1998	Multimedia Subcommittee Working Group. Interim Report on Technical Protection and Management.
December 1998	Multimedia Subcommittee Working Group. Final Report on Technical Protection and Management.

Contributors

Kanji Akahori received his Ph.D. in computer science and technology from Tokyo Institute of Technology, Tokyo, Japan. He is currently a professor in the Center of Research and Development of Educational Technology and the Department of Human System Science in the Graduate School of Decision Science and Technology in Tokyo Institute of Technology. He also teaches as a visiting professor at the University of the Air, the United Nations University in Tokyo, Japan. His research interests include information technology education, web-based learning systems, human–computer interaction, and language learning supporting systems. He has published numerous articles and books, including *Information Technology Education in Schools* (Gyosei, 2000), *Encyclopedia of Personal Computer* (Sywa, 2001), and *Computers and School* (NHK Books, 1994). He recently received the Outstanding Paper Award at the International Conference on Computers in Education in Taipei, Taiwan (2000).

Jim Cummins received his Ph.D. in 1974 from the University of Alberta, Edmonton, Alberta, Canada, in the area of educational psychology. He is currently a professor in the Department of Curriculum, Teaching and Learning in the Ontario Institute for Studies in Education of the University of Toronto, Toronto, Ontario, Canada. His research has focused on the nature of language proficiency and second language acquisition with particular emphasis on the social and educational barriers that limit academic success for culturally diverse students. He has also examined the role of technology in education in general and in second language learning in particular. His publications include: *Bilingualism and Special Education: Issues in Assessment and Pedagogy* (Multilingual Matters,

1984); (with Dennis Sayers) *Brave New Schools: Challenging Cultural Illiteracy through Global Learning Networks* (St. Martin's Press, 1995); and *Language, Power and Pedagogy: Bilingual Children in the Crossfire* (Multilingual Matters, 2000).

Masako Ogawa Douglas received her Ph.D. from the University of Southern California and was a lecturer of Japanese at University of California, Los Angeles. She is currently an assistant professor at California State University, Long Beach. Her research interests include instructed foreign language acquisition (primarily literacy development), foreign language instructional methodology, curriculum design, Japanese heritage learners' education (bi-literacy development and curriculum design), student-directed learning, technology in learning Japanese, and design of web placement tests. She has served as president of the Teachers of Japanese in Southern California. Her publications include *A Practical Guide to Learning Kanji for Learners from an Alphabetic Background* (McGraw-Hill, 2001, 2nd edition); "A Theme-Based Approach: Curriculum Design for Teaching an Advanced Course of Japanese as a Foreign Language," *Japanese-Language Education around the Globe* (The Japan Foundation Japanese Language Institute, 1996); "Japanese Cloze Tests: Towards their Construction" (ibid., 1994).

Yoshiko Kawamura is a professor at the School of Business and Commerce, Tokyo International University, Tokyo, Japan. She is currently teaching Japanese as a second language, intercultural communication, and linguistics at Tokyo International University and Waseda University. She is a visiting professor at the Institute of East Asian Studies, University of Vienna, from 2000 to 2002. Her research interests are in second language acquisition and computer-assisted instruction. She has recently been instrumental in the development of the Japanese Language Reading Tutorial System, "Reading Tutor," available through the internet (http://language.tiu.ac.jp).

Kazuko Nakajima is a professor of the Department of East Asian Studies at the University of Toronto, Toronto, Canada, where she teaches the Japanese language and Japanese language pedagogy to graduate students. Her research interests include computer-mediated distance education, heritage/minority language education, and Japanese-English bilingual education. She was the founding president of the Canadian Association for Japanese

Language Education, 1988–98. Her major publications include *KanjiCard* (a Hypercard computer program for learning basic 300 kanji) (Hahn Computer Institute, 1991), *Japanese as a Heritage Language—Canadian Experience* (CAJLE, 1997), *Bairingaru Kyoiku no Hoohoo* (Methodologies of Bilingual Education) (ALC, 1987, Revised 2001), and *Kaiwaryoku no Mikata to Hyouka* (The Oral Proficiency Assessment for Bilingual Children) (CAJLE, 2000).

Akifumi Oikawa is director of the Information Center for Education and Research at the Graduate University for Advanced Studies, where he has been a professor since 1994. He was a lecturer at the University of Tsukuba from 1975 to 1986, senior researcher at the National Institute for Educational Research from 1986 to 1991, and a professor at Ibaraki University from 1991 to 1994. He has published a number of articles on the use of computers in the humanities, especially in archaeology. He organized the CASTEL/J project in 1987 and since then he developed various kinds of databases which are useful for Japanese language teaching. One of them, the Komatsu Sakyo corpus which is the full-text database of all his works, is now available at the web site: <http://castelj.soken.ac.jp/groups/komatsu/>.

Hiroko Chinen Quackenbush received her Ph.D. in linguistics from the University of Michigan in 1970. From 1963 to 1975, she taught Japanese at the University of Michigan and Ohio State University, and from 1975 to 1987 she was at the University of Adelaide, Australia, and the Australian National University in Canberra. In 1987, she moved to Japan to become a professor at Hiroshima University. She later taught at Nagoya University, the International Christian University, and Nagoya University of Foreign Studies, where she is now professor of Japanese linguistics in the Graduate School of International Studies. Her main publications are *Gairaigo to Sono Kyouiku* (Formation and Teaching of Loan-words); "50-pun Hiragana Dounyuu-hoo: 'Rensou-hou' to 'Irotsuki Kaado-hou' no Hikaku" (Teaching Hiragana in 50 Minutes: Comparison of Teaching Methods using Association and Coloured Cards); and *Hiragana in 48 Minutes*. Her research interests include linguistics, loanwords, phonology, and Japanese language education.

Yuri Shimizu received her M.A. in applied linguistics from Columbia University's Teachers' College. From 1985 to 1995, she taught Japanese at the International Student Center, University of Tsukuba, and the University of Library and Information Science in Japan. In 1996, she became associate professor at the International Student Center, Kyushu University. Her principal publications are *Basic Kanji Book*, Vol. 1 and Vol. 2 (Bonjinsha, 1989); *Intermediate Kanji Book*, Vol. 1 and Vol. 2 (Bonjinsha, 1993, 2001); and *Nihongo Kyoshi no Tame no Kanji Shido Aidea Bukku* (A Resource Book of Kanji Instruction for Japanese Language Teachers) (Sotakusha, 1995). Her research interests are Japanese language education, kanji vocabulary instruction and acquisition of kanji vocabulary.

Yoko Suzuki received an M.A. in educational technology from the International Christian University (ICU) in Japan in 1985. She taught Japanese language at ICU as a part-time instructor from 1984 to 1989 and has been a full-time instructor since 1989. Her main publications include "Overview of Japanese Language Education and Research Using Computers" and *Japanese for College Students: Basic* (Kodansha International, 1996). Her research interests are Japanese language education and development of systems for independent study of the Japanese language using computers.

Yasu-Hiko Tohsaku is professor at the University of California, San Diego, where he is the director of the Language Program at the Graduate School of International Relations and Pacific Studies, and the coordinator of the Undergraduate Japanese Language Program. He received his Ph.D. in linguistics from the University of California, San Diego, in 1983. He is the author of numerous articles on second language acquisition and Japanese language pedagogy. His beginning and intermediate Japanese language textbooks, *Yookoso!* (McGraw-Hill) have been used throughout the world. He is the chair of the Professional Development Committee of the Association of Teachers of Japanese (U.S.A.) and a member of the executive board of the Collaborative Project on the National Standards for Learning Foreign Languages.

Michio Tsutsui is director of the Technical Japanese Program at the University of Washington, Seatle, an associate professor in the Department of Technical Communication, and the Donald E. Petersen Professor in the College of Engineering. Before he joined the University of Washington in 1990, he taught the Japanese language at the University of California at Davis, the Middlebury Summer School, and Massachusetts Institute of Technology (MIT).

He also taught Japanese linguistics at the University of California at Davis and Josai International University in Japan. At MIT, he also jointly established and taught in the Summer Intensive Technical Japanese Program. Tsutsui's research areas include technology for language learning, second language acquisition, and Japanese for special purposes. His major publications include *A Dictionary of Basic Japanese Grammar* (The Japan Times, 1986) and *A Dictionary of Intermediate Japanese Grammar* (with Seiichi Makino) (The Japan Times, 1995). He earned a Ph.D. in linguistics from the University of Illinois at Urbana-Champaign.

Hilofumi Yamamoto is research fellow of the Graduate School of International Relations and Pacific Studies, University of California, San Diego. He was assistant professor of the Institute of Literature and Linguistics, International Student Center, University of Tsukuba, Ibaragi, Japan. He was a teacher of Japanese and a network manager and programmer of the International Student Center, University of Tsukuba, 1992–2000. He received the 1995 Society of Japan Science Education Prize. He produced the video *Situational Functional Japanese* Vols. 1–3 (Japan Cinesell Co. Ltd.) and the JACOP Database Project. His major interest is Japanese language teaching methods and psychology. His publications include "Analysis of Japanese Sentence Comprehension using Immediate Response Methods," *Papers of Japanese Language Teaching*, 1999; "Evaluation Methods of a System for Reading Technical Texts," *Journal of Japanese Language Teaching*, 1995; and "The Effect of Signaling in Scientific and Technical Passages in Japanese (1) The Case for Native Readers," *Journal of Science Education*, 1994.

Index

Academic Japanese and Applications Project (PROJ), 70
academic language learning, viii, xi, xv, xvii, 25-97, 109, 111, 123–43, 145, 151, 166
American Council for Teaching of Foreign Languages (ACTFL), xi, 90, 96
Apple Canada Education Foundation, ix
Apple Centre for Innovation in East Asian Languages, ix
assessment of students, 43, 55, 146, 149, 162
    See also: tests and quizzes
assignments: *See* homework
audiolingual and audiovisual instruction, x, 1–3, 15, 114, 124, 141
audiotapes, 123–44, 148
authors' rights, 182–4
autonomy: *See* individualized learning

Berne Treaty Concerning the Protection of the Written Work, 179
bilingualism, developing, 166
Breen, Jim, 158
browsers: *See* web browsers

CALL: *See* Computer-Assisted Language Learning
CASTEL/J: *See* Computer Assisted System of Teaching and Learning/Japanese
CATERS: *See* Computer Assisted TEchnical Reading System
CD-ROMs, xvii
    CASTEL/J materials on, x, 70, 83, 173, 175, 183, 186
    closed programs on, 32–3, 119
    disseminating teaching materials on, 22, 29, 108, 186
    film material on, 7–8
    multimedia systems on, 105, 119
Center for Research on Evaluation, Standards and Student Testing, UCLA, 162
Cha-Sen morphological parser, 72–3, 85,
checkers: *See* error analysis and correction; grammar
Chinese
    as heritage language, 145
    multimedia system for reading, 126
classroom teaching, xvi, 99
cloze procedures and tests, 108–9, 114
comic strips, as teaching tools, xvi, 10, 15–19
communication: *See* conversational skills; writing skills
composition: *See* writing skills

Computer-Assisted Language Learning (CALL) software, development of, 25–37

Computer Assisted System of Teaching and Learning/Japanese (CASTEL/J) database, x, xviii, 44–5, 47, 70, 71, 83, 124, 141, 173–89
Research Group, vii–ix, xviii, 141

Computer Assisted TEchnical Reading System (CATERS), 124

computers, use in instruction, xvi, 20, 71
calculation system, xvi
client-server systems, xvi, 41–70, 97
disadvantages, 148–9, 164–5
skill in using, need for, 8
See also: error analysis and correction; software

concordances, 47

conferences
Pavia, ix
Toronto, vii–x

conversational skills
assessment, 89–91, 94–6, 98–9
enhancement, xvi–xvii, 4, 26, 34–5, 43, 107–8, 119, 123, 146, 148, 150–51
See also: speech comprehension

Copyright Counci,l 179

copyright issues, x–xi, xviii, 8, 15–16, 22, 45–6, 173–89

Copyright Research and Information Center (CRIC), 179

critical language awareness, developing, 112

curricula, 174
customizing, 145–6
design and development, xvi, 41, 43, 110, 145–6, 156–7, 162
fixed or pre-existing, disadvantages of, 10, 33, 156

databases, instructional, ix, xi, xvi, xviii, 15–16, 28, 57, 61, 63, 71–2
compared and evaluated, 41–70
copyright protection, 180–85
See also: Computer Assisted System of Teaching and Learning/Japanese; kanji

DejaVu, 43, 50, 52–3

dialogues, practice, 151

dictionaries, 107
bilingual versus unilingual, merits of, 116–20
online, xvii–xviii, 12, 45–6, 49–50, 69, 72, 83–5, 105, 108, 110, 112, 119, 124–5, 127, 130–33, 141, 157, 160, 163–4, 174–6

DictLinker, 124

e-Lective Language Learning system, xvii, 106–20
e-mail, 91
  for bilingual exchanges between students, viii–ix, 25, 148, 151–2, 156,
    162
  for disseminating teaching materials and tools, 43, 47, 50
  for reports to teachers, 41, 55
  in Japanese, sending, 150–51, 155
  See also: Internet
English as a second language, xv, 111, 113–14
  difficulties of learning, 107–8
error analysis and correction, xvi, 11–12, 58, 63, 98–9, 151

feedback: *See* assessment; self-teaching and self-assessment
field tests, xvii, 123, 127–30
films and videos, as teaching materials, xvi, 4–5, 7–9, 13, 20, 25–9, 34–5,
    45, 70, 148, 175
Foreign Service Institute (FSI), U.S. State Department, viii, xi, 94, 100
formal registers: *See* respect language
furigana: *See* kanji

glossaries: *See* dictionaries
grammar, 84, 98–9, 107, 119, 123, 151
  computer checking and support, xvi, 12, 43, 54–63, 70, 72, 105, 110,
    174
  English grammar assessment, 55
  self-assessment, 95–6
  self-tutorial, xvi, 43, 57–62, 70, 109–10

Hatasa, Kazumi, 49
heritage language, learning Japanese as, xii, xv, xvii–xviii, 145–69
hiragana: *See* kana
homework, 55, 60–63, 97, 146, 148
honorific registers: *See* respect language
human resources, 63–4, 72
hungul, 91
hypermedia, 2

individualized learning, xv, xvii, 105–12, 114, 145–69
  See also: self-teaching and self-assessment
instructional tools: *See* teaching tools
Intelligent Tutoring System (ITS), 2–3
interactive learning systems, x, 2–4, 8–12, 16, 28, 32
  for instructors, 34

Interagency Language Round Table (ILR), U.S. State Department, xii, xvii, 89, 97, 100
Internet 25
  as source of teaching materials, 13, 20–21, 41, 47, 108, 148, 150
  as teaching tool, 146, 156, 163–4
  dictionary on, 124
  disseminating teaching resources on, ix, xvi, 1, 10, 13, 49, 72–3, 175, 186
  ethics of sharing resources on, x, 186–7
  Japanese communication on, 150
  multimedia systems on, 1
  reading text on, 151, 154–5
  searching and updating sites, time spent on, 165
  self-assessment, use for, xv, xvii, 89–102
  software development, effect on, 175
  See also: e-mail
interviews, 149, 152, 162
ITS: *See* Intelligent Tutoring System

JACOP S/F/DB, 45, 65
Japanese Keyword in Context (JKWIC), 43, 47–8, 70
Japanese language
  computer analysis, 11–12
  difficulty of learning, viii, xi–xii. *See also:* kanji
  gender in, 156
  proficiency test. *See under* Japan Foundation
  use as foreign language, xii
  writing style, versus English, xiv, 146
  writing system xii. *See also* hungul; kana; kanji; romaji
  See also: respect language
Japan Forum, 175
Japan Foundation xii
  Language Proficiency Test, xvi–xvii, 71–3, 75, 79, 82–5, 123
Japan Industrial Standards (JIS), 176
JKWIC: *See* Japanese Keyword in Context
journals, to record students' progress, 162
JUPITER, 72
JWPCE, 148, 157–63, 166

kana, xii–xiii, 10, 13, 19–20, 25, 46, 50, 91
kanji, x, xii–xiv, 13, 46, 50, 53, 69–70, 91, 125, 156
  advantages, alleged, 148
  audiotapes as help with learning, 126–8, 133–5, 148
  customized readings for kanji-background students, 126
  dictionaries, 124–5, 127, 157–8, 160, 163–4, 176

difficulty of learning, ix, xiii–xiv, xvii, 19, 76, 80–82, 147–8, 164
frequency counter, 160, 164
furigana, 72, 84, 136, 148
grammatical usage, 153
Kanji Counter, 85
kanji-hiragana conversion program, xvi, 10, 19–20
Kanji-Level Checker (KLC), xvi–xvii, 71–85
learning software, ix, 43, 61, 63–5, 69–70, 72, 124, 159–61, 166
learning strategies, 147, 149–50, 152–3, 155
radicals, learning, 147, 153, 157
recognition, 25, 54, 61, 63, 76
reference filters, 46, 69–70
searcher, 164
statistics filter (ksf), 69
strokes, number and order of, xiii, 141, 156–7, 176
teaching, xvi, 58, 60–63, 65, 146–65
tests, 147, 149–50, 155, 162–3, 166
katakana: *See* kana
keigo: *See* respect language
Komatsu, Sakyo 70

language learning issues and methods, 2, 10–11, 25, 16, 104, 109,
   113–18, 149–50, 166
Language Partner (Nihongo Partner), xvi, 26–9, 37
learning strategies, 123, 130–31, 135–6, 140, 147, 149, 174
   supports, xvii, 105, 112, 115
listening comprehension: *See* speech comprehension
literacy: *See* reading skills; writing skills
literature, online, 45, 50
local area network (LAN), 3, 41

machine translation, 25
Mailgloss, 43, 49–51
Mailing Forum of the Japanese Network 155
microcomputers, xv, 25, 126, 157, 173, 175
multimedia systems, ix, xvi, 1, 3–22, 25, 110, 119, 141, 175
   Chinese reading, for, 126
   comic strips, xvi, 10, 15–19
   copyright issues, 179
   customizing, 21–2, 33
   design, 5, 112
   digital courseware, ix
   films and videos, xvi, 4–5, 7–9, 13, 20, 25–9, 34–5, 45, 70, 148, 175
   graphic organizers, 105
   news programs, 46, 49

pictures, 45, 70, 141, 176
recordings, 43, 45, 176
television dramas, 46
versus text, 4–7
See also: audiolingual and audiovisual instruction; audiotapes
Multimedia Research Project, 7

National Institute for Educational Research, Tokyo, 71, 173, 187
National Standards for Learning Foreign Languages, U.S., 89
native speakers, learners' interaction with, viii, 107, 148, 151–2
natural language processing (NLP) techniques, 10–11, 25
network society, language learning in, x–xi, xvi, 1–37
newspaper articles, as teaching tools, 50, 91, 152, 156, 164–5, 175
    common kanji in, 161
news programs, as teaching tools, 46, 49
N-gram, 43, 48–9
Nihongo-cali (Japanese Computer-Assisted Language Instruction), 11
Nihongo Partner: *See* Language Partner
novels, as teaching tools, 50, 70

oral communication: *See* conversational skills
oral interviews: *See* interviews

Paris Agreement Concerning the Protection of Industrial Property, 179
personal computers: *See* microcomputers
phonetic (phonological) supports: *See* pronunciation aids
pictures, as teaching tools, 45, 70, 141, 176
portfolios, as teaching tools, 150–55, 162, 164
pre-university students
    Japanese for, xv, 19, 85
    textbooks for, 78–80, 86
printed texts, learning through, 105–22, 135, 145, 156–7, 161
    online versions, 174
pronunciation aids, xvii, 119, 126-8, 131, 133–5, 147, 176

quizzes: *See* tests and quizzes

reading skills
    assessment, 89–91, 97
    audiotaped models, xvii, 123–43
    comprehension, xvii–xviii, 72, 114, 123, 126–8, 131–40, 151
    development, 108, 111–15, 127, 145
    independent practice, xv, 105–69
    materials, 162
    speed, xvii, 114, 126–30, 133–6

tests, 85
time spent developing, 156–7
See also: printed texts
recordings, as teaching tools, 43, 45, 176
reports, for teachers, 41, 55
respect language, learning, xii, xviii, 13–16, 98, 128, 146–8, 151, 155, 163–4, 177
role-playing, as teaching tool, 148, 155
romaji, xii, 11
Rosenthal, Glen, 157, 166

self-teaching and self-assessment, xv–xvii, 12–13, 28, 32, 34, 41, 43, 57–62, 65, 73–8, 89–144, 149
Shinsho Library, 71, 83, 123–43
Side Treaty on Rights in Intellectual Property (TRIPS), 180
Simple Mail Transport Protocol (SMTP) server system, 49
Society for Teaching Japanese as a Foreign Language, 7
software
    collaboration in designing, need for, xi, xvi, 26, 35–6, 187
    design and development, xv–xvi, 1–37, 173–5
    dissemination, xvi, 26, 29, 34–5, 157, 175, 186–7
    evaluation, 5, 20–22, 26, 29–34, 41–64, 69–70
    user-friendliness, importance of, 30–32, 112
Software Engineering Foundation, 13
speech comprehension, 8, 16, 25, 43, 46, 89–91, 98–9, 123, 130, 133–4, 136, 151
    See also: conversational skills
standards-based instruction, 89
Standards for Foreign Language Learning, 150
students
    aptitude and readiness to learn, 64
    assessment, 43, 55–6, 146, 149, 162. *See also* tests and quizzes
    autonomy: *See* individualized learning; self-teaching and self-assessment
    computer access and skills, need for, 8, 148–9, 164–5
    critical language awareness of, developing, 112
    French proficiency of English-speaking Canadian students, 107
    kanji-background students, special materials for, 126
    learning environments, 174
    learning strategies: *See* learning strategies
    native speakers, need to interact with, viii, 107, 148, 151–2
    peer contact, importance of, viii–ix, 25, 148, 151–2, 156, 162
    portfolios, use of, 150–55, 162, 164
    pre-university students, xv, 19, 78–80, 82, 85
    strategic competence, developing, 150
syllabuses: *See* curricula

teaching tools, xv–xvi, 41–88
    customizing, 21–2, 33, 109
    See also: Internet; multimedia systems; portfolios; printed texts; software; textbooks
technical terms, identifying, 47
television dramas, as teaching tools, 46
tests and quizzes, 41, 43, 54–8, 63, 65, 72, 85, 89–94, 97–100, 109, 114, 117-18, 127-8, 139–40, 149, 152, 155, 162, 174–5
textbooks, 20, 174–5
    copyright law, 186
    evaluation, xvi, 4, 71–88
texts: *See* printed texts
touch typing, difficulty of, in Japanese, xv
translation: *See* machine translation
treaties, 179–80
TRIPS: *See* Side Treaty on Rights in Intellectual Property

University of California at Los Angeles (UCLA), 146–7, 157, 162, 166

videoconferencing viii
videos: *See* films and videos
vocabulary, 46, 125
    checking, 54, 70, 72–3, 98–9, 117–18, 173; self-assessment 76
    development, 60–63, 72, 105, 107, 110, 120, 136–7
    difficulty, assessing, xvi–xvii, 50, 73
    learning in context, merits of, 117
    lists, usefulness of, 152, 154, 157, 159, 161–2
    teaching, merits of, 114–19
Vocabulary Level Checker (VLC), xvi–xvii, 71–85

web browsers, use of, 12, 15–16, 47, 55, 97, 175, 187
white papers, government, as learning materials, 175
Wordgloss, 49
work, definition of, 180–82
workshops, ix
World Intellectual Property Organization (WIPO), United Nations, 179–80
writing skills
    assessment, 89–90
    computer-assisted courses, ix, 10, 54, 65, 70
    correspondence, 151
    development, viii–ix, 108, 111, 145–6, 151
    See also: hungul; kana; kanji; romaji